Windows on Salvation

Windows on Salvation

Edited by

Donald English

DARTON · LONGMAN + TODD

First published 1994 by
Darton, Longman and Todd Ltd
1 Spencer Court
140–142 Wandsworth High Street
London SW18 4JJ

ISBN 0–232–52038–0

A catalogue record for this book is available
from the British Library

Phototypeset by Intype, London SW19 8DR
Printed and bound in Great Britain
at Page Bros, Norwich

Contents

Part 3: The Modern Challenge

Notes on Contributors

Dr BEVERLEY CLACK lectures in the Philosophy of Religion and Modern Theology at Roehampton Institute. Her main interest is feminist philosophy of religion and she is currently working on two books in this field. She is a member of the Methodist Church and part of a group set up by the Home Missions Division to consider issues of apologetics.

The Revd Dr JOHN W. DRANE is Director of the Centre for the Study of Christianity and Contemporary Society at the University of Stirling, and author of a number of books on Christian faith, the most recent being *Evangelism for a New Age: Creating Churches for the Next Century*. Both he and his wife have extensive involvement in the ecumenical movement, in Britain and internationally.

Professor DUNCAN B. FORRESTER is Professor of Christian Ethics and Practical Theology and Principal of New College in the University of Edinburgh. He is also Director of the Centre for Theology and Public Issues. Before coming to Edinburgh he served as an educational missionary in South India, and as Chaplain and Lecturer at the University of Sussex. He is married, with two children. Among his books are *Theology and Politics* and *Beliefs, Values and Policies: Conviction Politics in a Secular Age*.

Canon Dr SEHON GOODRIDGE is the first Principal of The Simon of Cyrene Theological Institute in London. Formerly Principal of Codrington College in Barbados, and Senior Lecturer in the University of the West Indies, Cave Hill Campus. He has written extensively and served on the Inter-Anglican Theological and Doctrinal Commission which produced the Report *For the Sake of the Kingdom.* He is an Examining Chaplain to the Bishop of Southwark, a member of the Synod Board for Social Responsibility and Chaplain to the Queen.

The Revd Dr MICHAEL GREEN is currently a member of the Springboard initiative and Adviser in Evangelism to the Archbishops of Canterbury and York. Originally an academic, he is primarily an evangelist and leads missions and training courses in the UK and overseas.

The Revd Dr ALISTER E. MCGRATH is Research Lecturer in Systematic Theology at Oxford University, Professor of Systematic Theology at Regent College, Vancouver, and Lecturer at Wycliffe Hall, Oxford. A priest in the Church of England, he is also Consultant Editor of *Christianity Today* and serves on the International Commission for Reformed Theology.

The Revd Dr ROBINSON MILWOOD was the first black West Indian to be appointed Circuit Superintendent Minister in the Methodist Church. A pioneer in educational and theological empowerment of the poor through the Stoke Newington Mission Educational Institute, he is also Senior part-time Lecturer in Religious Studies at Birkbeck College, University of London, and Academic Tutor in Theology and Philosophy at Greenwich University.

MICHAEL RICHARDS is a Canon of Westminster Cathedral and is especially occupied in ecumenism. He has been Editor of *The Clergy Review,* Lecturer in Church History at St Edmund's College, Ware and Heythrop College, University of London, and parish priest of St Mary's, Chelsea. He is a member of the Methodist/Roman Catholic International Commission.

The Revd Dr JOHN B. TAYLOR is General Secretary of the Methodist Church Division of Ministries, with especial responsibility for Ministerial Training. In addition to his circuit experience as a minister, he has been University Chaplain in Sheffield and Tutor in Systematic Theology at the Queen's College in Birmingham.

The Revd JOHN MUNSEY TURNER is Superintendent Minister of the Methodist Circuit in Bolton. He was formerly University Chaplain in Leeds and Lecturer in Church History at the Queen's College in Birmingham. His books include *Introducing Theology, Conflict and Reconciliation (Studies in Methodism and Ecumenism)* and *Preaching through the Christian Year.*

FRANCES YOUNG is Edward Cadbury Professor of Theology and Head of the Department of Theology at the University of Birmingham. She is also a Methodist minister and the mother of three now adult sons, one of whom has severe mental and physical disabilities. She has written a number of books, including *Face to Face*, a theological reflection on her family experience.

Preface

The Decade of Evangelism was an idea which might have been expected to receive universal affirmation from Christians around the world. Instead it raised a whole set of questions. Did it mean that professional evangelists would simply step up their activities and get more work? Would a new generation of evangelists be recruited on the strength of the idea? Would that branch of the Church which had always emphasised evangelism now come into its own? And if this was to be the Decade of Evangelism, are all the other decades not so? Whatever the Christian Church can be properly blamed for, it isn't a failure to criticise the ideas coming from within its own ranks!

Yet in a curious way this bevy of questions, and others, has in itself provided some of the impetus for the Decade. Christians from different parts of the Church have argued their corner and shown that they too are committed to evangelism, if not always in a traditional way. More local churches every year are putting evangelism on to their agenda. And there is a much greater willingness to work together across the denominational boundaries in order to share the Christian message with those outside. Even the difference of meaning between evangelism (stressing the proclamation of the gospel) and evangelisation (emphasising the planting of the gospel at the heart of every sector of society) has quickened understanding and produced a more wholesome view of what the task involves.

This book makes a modest attempt to go behind those questions and their answers. It asks not so much about *how* the good news is to be offered, but *what* is the good news that is being offered. It is less about context and method and more about content. In order to focus that question we have taken the biblical theme of salvation.

The title *Windows on Salvation* is meant to indicate a variety of viewpoints on offer. Each writer takes a particular area of expertise as a vantage point from which to view salvation. They were also asked to present the material from a personal point of view, so that something of themselves may be perceived in the content and the way they offer it. None of the writers was expected to affirm what the others wrote. In one sense each window stands in its own right. Yet what emerges here is a fascinating picture, with remarkable inner unity as well as a refreshing variety of perspective and conclusion.

There was no great attempt to get an exactly balanced team of authors in terms of denomination and theology, experience and status, gender and race, though readers will note a fairly balanced group nevertheless. But I invited the people whom I believed would best write for this book; people who are respected in their field of expertise, who write with perception and conviction, and who have the ability through what they write to stimulate and encourage others. I am personally most grateful to them for so readily agreeing to be part of this endeavour.

Through this book Darton, Longman and Todd offers a theological contribution to the Decade of Evangelism. The hope is that all who wish to understand more deeply the meaning of the Christian gospel will find its varied insights satisfying and stimulating.

DONALD ENGLISH

Introduction

Donald English

Salvation is what Christianity is about. John the Baptist's father, Zechariah, recognised how much more was happening than simply the birth to him and Elizabeth of an unusual child (Luke 1:67–79). He saw this event as a preparation for the deliverance from enemies promised by the prophets. It was called salvation. But this young baby would also teach God's people, giving them a knowledge of salvation, interpreted as forgiveness of sins through God's mercy. From the very beginning of the Christian story salvation was a mixture of physical and spiritual well-being.

The same combination is clear when Jesus uses the word salvation. He called the tax-gatherer Zacchaeus down from the tree where he was hiding and invited himself to Zacchaeus' house. Eventually his host confessed his wrongs and promised to repay four times over and give half of his possessions to the poor. Jesus greeted the promise with the words 'Today, salvation has come to this house' (Luke 19:1–10). Physical and spiritual changes had taken place.

The early Christians also were convinced that salvation was at the centre of what they were called to preach. When questioned about their new-found mission and asked to account for it. Peter replied in words that were both startling and offensive to those who first heard them. Referring to the healing of a disabled beggar (Acts 4:10,12), Peter said, 'It is by the name of Jesus Christ of Nazareth, whom you crucified but whom God raised from the dead, that this man stands before you healed ... Salvation is found in no one else, for there is no other name under heaven given to men by which we must be saved.' (Acts 3:1–10).

Paul is equally clear in giving his reason for preaching. In

1

justifying to his readers in Rome the mission he was engaged in he writes, 'I am not ashamed of the gospel, because it is the power of God for the salvation of everyone who believes' (Romans 1:16). The rest of his letter to the Romans spelled out what that meant. It is certainly about how God in Christ deals with the problem of human sinfulness. It is a profoundly spiritual issue. But it is also about the way in which those who are saved will live the whole of their lives (Romans 1:17).

Salvation is about the whole of the believer's life from the moment of commitment right through to beyond death. In the First Letter of Peter, the readers, many of whom were probably slaves with few worldly possessions or comforts, are given a reminder of what their Christian faith means to them. Peter writes of a salvation 'ready to be revealed in the last time' (1 Peter 1:5), a pointing forward to the end of the world and the revealing of Christ as Lord of all. But a little later he reminds them that they are already 'receiving the goal of your faith, the salvation of your souls' (1 Peter 1:9). It is fully realised at the end, but they are already experiencing it now.

The question for us, assuming that we still see salvation as being at the heart of the Christian message, is how we are to understand, interpret and commend it today. Our world is so very different from that of the first-century Roman Empire. To put it another way, 'From what does our world need to be saved and what does the Christian gospel have to offer to enable our world to be saved?' The writers of this book address this question in some detail.

I offer here some introductory reflections, based on what I see and hear around me in the world today.

The international scene is politically highly unstable. The struggle between the two great powers – the USA and the USSR – was rightly seen as a threat to world peace. But in fact it also offered a large degree of stability so long as it did not erupt into war. All the nations of the world knew where they stood by judging their position in relation to one or other of the two rivals. Many conflicts at world level were settled by the mutual influence, often against one another in a balancing way, of the two giants. But that compelling contest, occupying centre stage in the world's affairs is no longer there to concentrate our attention. The USSR has broken up into its several parts and faces an enormous economic task of self-renewal. In a curious way the United States of America is somehow weakened by the lack of a single foreign threat. Instability is the result.

Partly as a response to this new situation, the nations of the world are searching for new power blocks. Great Britain is enduring a good deal of political pain over the issue of our part in the new Europe which is emerging. The United States is strengthening its ties with Canada and Mexico. The countries of Asia are steadily building up relationships of trade and mutual strength. The so-called south-eastern Pacific rim nations could well become the economic centre of the next decade. There is already talk of the distant regeneration of the continent of Africa if only South Africa can succeed in its new-found political freedom. But this time of searching for new alliances is an uncertain time for the world.

We might feel that the two movements described above could lead to a more stable world in the long run and therefore be patient with the intervening uncertainty. But other forces are threatening even that promise for the future. A combination of geographical location, tribal loyalty and political commitment is producing forms of national consciousness which slip not only into nationalism, but still worse into racism. If some form of reactionary religion can be added to the mixture then we have the most deadly potion of all. The Middle East and Ireland provide two sad examples of this process. Bosnia, with its ethnic cleansing, is sharper still in its contours of hatred and destruction.

At the same time the United Nations is struggling to hold its standing and reputation among the nations of the world. It doesn't have the permanent force to create an international police force. It has to depend on the generosity of the richer nations to sustain any initiative. Many of the weaker nations feel that there is a certain elitism about the way the United Nations works and about the issues it is willing to deal with and those which it seems able to neglect. It can commend peace; it can try to protect peace, or even enable it, but it can't enforce it. In many situations in the world 'might' still seems to be 'right'.

If we were seeing a steady increase in the meeting of some of the basic needs of the developing parts of the world we might feel we could ride the storm of political unrest. But that doesn't seem to be the picture. In his account of this situation Paul Kennedy points out in particular the danger facing the world because of the population crisis which grows worse.[1] The over-populating nations are still over-populating; the under-populating nations are still under-populating. The latter will solve their problem by use of technology which reduces the need for a large work force. But this is the worst news of all for the over-populated world, which needs more work, not less, for its increasing numbers. The rich becoming richer and the poor becoming poorer is thus a growing reality at world level. As richer nations more effectively close their borders to refugees and immigrants the room for manoeuvre and improvement is denied to the vast populations of the developing world. Paul Kennedy is not convinced that the powerful nations have the will or the desire to do enough to improve the situation.

There is a further question which relates particularly to western cultures but which, through them, influences the rest of the world. It has to do with the effect of rationalism on the development of our civilisation. Sometimes referred to as the Enlightenment, it was a movement of thought most clearly seen originating in the eighteenth century, with a strong emphasis on the power of human reason to observe, describe, organise and use the resources of the world and the meaning behind them. Our scientific and technological advances depend on this conviction about the power of reason. None could doubt the enormous advantages accruing to humanity through this revolution of insight, discovery and subsequent technological advance.

We are now possibly facing a new turning point, however.[2] In some areas of our scientific, and particularly medical, discovery the nature of the opportunities or the dangers ahead requires more than scientific knowledge for a right judgement to be reached. It is increasingly common for those making discoveries or describing possibilities for the future to point out that whether or not we go down that line is not a decision for the scientist to take. It is for society to decide what kind of world it wants for the future, what kind of world it wishes to build. The implication is that the purely rational approach to life may not be enough to determine what we should do about the results of this approach to the universe around it. Taking eggs that will not produce an embryo and making it possible for them to produce a life is a simple example of the problem. By which criteria are we to answer that question?

If we shift our attention to our national life the problems do not diminish. Because of our technological society we have more possessions and aids to living than any other generation. One might well expect, having read about any previous age in our national existence, that we would be a more contented population than at any time in the history of Britain. Yet we are far from that situation. The government of the day faces threats to society from almost every quarter.

Crime is on the increase. Younger and younger people feature in the criminal courts. There is great concern about the rise in violence in our society and in its possible sources. Drug-taking is still on the increase, as is the number of suicides each year. The family is less and less able to take the strain of modern life-styles. Fifty per cent of our marriages end in divorce. Numbers of the homeless are on the increase. Trickle-down does not seem to provide for the needy because those who are not needy are too anxious about their own future, or unconcerned about those in need, to trickle enough down. Politicians adjust their policies to promise us a maximum of possessions. To include in a manifesto a proposal to increase tax, even for good purposes, is generally viewed as a way to lose elections. We give the impression of being a dissatisfied people, for all our modern gadgets, aids and possessions.

Of course the story is not a wholly bad one. The living standards in general in our country are a vast improvement on previous ages. Large amounts of money are given for special appeals. More people have holidays and travel abroad. The medical care available today is far in excess of anything in previous centuries. Housing is, again in general, far better than anything we have known in the past. Possibilities of communication are breath-takingly different for us today; so are the forms of entertainment available, many in our own homes. Yet we are not a happy people, or a contented people, or a liberated people. We seem to be grown in upon ourselves and helpless to set ourselves free. Our frustration is vented upon others whom we blame – the government, or failure of law and order, or the family, or the education system, or single-parent families, or immigrants. We do not present a pretty picture.

It is one thing to offer a picture of the situation. Diagnoses are two-a-penny. Much more difficult is the task of offering some way out of the dilemma we face. The Christian Church must avoid the temptation of the simple solution. A sound-bite culture longs for the 'thirty-second' answer to every problem. Christians have often responded by sticking biblical texts on problems, as though that somehow solved them. But Christians should be the very last to fall for that kind of approach, since our testimony is to the way God created a wonderfully complex and endlessly awe-inspiring universe. We are not here to make everything clear in any simplistic way. Part of the Christian witness is to the essential mystery of life. The question is not whether we have a collection of ready answers to all problems, but whether we have the materials from which ways of addressing the issues can be found. I believe – and this book is written in the conviction – that such materials do exist within the Christian faith.

Christians have a doctrine of Creation, for example. It is not, as we now see more clearly, primarily about *how* the world came into being. It is about *why* it came into being. It is about God's love being extended to what emerged in the creation. It is about a good purpose for everything, about the heart of the universe being personal and not simply power. It involves our answerability as human beings: answerable to God for everything around us and particularly answerable for one another. It means that what we have is not ours by right. We have possessions in stewardship from God. With the gifts we are given we are called to be co-creators with God of the world he desires.

Then there is the doctrine of Incarnation. It is about help being given neither by message nor by good advice from a distance, but by the helper coming alongside those in need. The birth and ministry, the dying and rising and ascending of Jesus Christ provide us with both a commentary and a model. They are a commentary on how our world is meant to work. And they are a model for our way of relating to one another in seeking to work with God in it. Jesus Christ lived with the constant sense that everything happened under the loving eye of God his father. He saw time as of significance because of its relation to eternity. He looked not so much on the outward achievements as the inner condition of a person. He did not encourage the helping hand to those in need but the giving of oneself. He pointed out that the search for happiness somehow always ends in frustration, but that the search for goodness produces happiness. Above all he showed that God's way of lowly suffering love for the needy is the strongest power in the world. He rose from the dead.

Then there is the doctrine of Redemption. It is about the possibility of repentance, true change of heart. It is about the chance of conversion, true change of direction. We can be forgiven and we can begin again. Individuals and families, companies and nations, can change their minds and their directions, accepting that a previous way has been wrong. A new start is always possible.

There is a doctrine of Judgement, too. We sow what we reap. God has made the world to operate on a moral basis which we flout at our cost. It can be argued that we found many health-giving freedoms in the 1960s in our culture. But we claimed one freedom too many – freedom from God's way and authority. Once that over-arching accountability is thrown out we find that the rest of the system begins to crumble. Each separate part – whether relationships, sex or money, work or leisure, government or media – is expected to bear a weight it cannot carry. Becoming the real source of our dependence, these things achieve a status of idolatry which steadily leads us into imprisonment and bondage. When we reap what we have sown we begin to look for scapegoats, blaming the very areas of life which we have wrested out of their proper place of subservience to God's purposes.

And there is Trinity. Often wrestled with as a problem of belief, Trinity is also about perfect living in relationship. It is about a way of being for mutual care and love, which offers itself for the need of others, for their salvation.

These Christian doctrines have fulfilled many functions in their time. They provide the basis on which the Christian family, for all its internal differences, can find common ground in frequent affirmation in public worship. They have often served like the white lines in the centre of the road during the dark nights of the Church's journey through history. They have stretched the intellect and the imagination of the most profound thinkers, while offering guidance and support for the simplest believers.

The question now to be faced – and addressed in a variety of ways in this book – is whether a faith based on such premises can still offer salvation, even in a world as exciting, rapidly changing, and often frightening as our own. Those of us who have written in these pages believe it can, and invite those who will to join us in the journey.

Part 1

The Received Tradition

1 Salvation in the Hebrew Scriptures*

John B. Taylor

Omnibus words

The message of the Methodist Church, according to *A Catechism for the use of the people called Methodists,* may be summarised as:

> All need to be saved.
> All may be saved.
> All may know themselves saved.
> All may be saved to the uttermost.

Salvation is a central concept in defining the faith of the Methodist Church, as it is in defining the faith of the Church universal, for that same document goes on to describe it as 'the forgiveness of our sin, deliverance from guilt, and the gift of new life in Christ'. For Christians, salvation is not something to be defined in the abstract. It is centred on the Jesus who lived in Nazareth and who came to be recognised as the Christ, God's anointed king. Salvation is not one simple occurrence. It is a process. It has a past, a present and a future tense (cf. Ephesians 2:5; 1 Corinthians 1:18; Romans 5:9). It is something to be experienced. It is itself a multi-layered word, rich in meaning, usually defined by the situation or context of those in need. It is for each one of us, whoever we are. It is for all, wherever we might be.

For the descendants of those who were once slaves in Egypt and exiles in Babylon salvation has a different reference point. It centres on the God who delivers his people from bondage and from captivity. It is he who makes them a people, who were not a people. It is he who gathers them together, those who were scattered far and wide. Salvation is focused on experience of the Exodus and the return from Exile.

> I will sing to the Lord, for he has triumphed gloriously; horse and rider he has thrown into the sea. The Lord is my strength and my might, and he has become my salvation ... (Exodus 15:1b–2a).

> I will strengthen the house of Judah, and I will save the house of Joseph. I will bring them back because I have compassion on them, and they shall be as though I had not rejected them; for I am the Lord their God and I will answer them. (Zechariah 10:6)

It is first and foremost a community concept. The descendants of Abraham and Sarah, of Moses and Miriam, of those who returned from Babylon, found their identity together, in covenant with Yahweh. For many within the Jewish community down the ages it has had, and for many still has, strong associations with the land God promised to Abraham.

Furthermore, as well as being itself a multi-layered word in both its Jewish and its Christian settings, salvation is also a part of a broad semantic field. It belongs to a cluster of ideas which cannot in the end be considered in separation from each other. Words like covenant and lovingkindness, righteousness and justice, blessing and peace are all windows on salvation. Each in itself has been the subject of scholarly study. Nevertheless, to appreciate their interconnectedness and to feel something of the rich texture of salvation, it is important to review this network of kindred ideas and overlapping concepts, none of which in Hebrew thought is ever a mere abstraction, for, fascinating as linguistic studies often are, it is the context not the etymology of words which is decisive in establishing their meaning. Covenant and lovingkindness, righteousness and justice, blessing and peace are the back-cloth against which the process of salvation is played out. It is usually possible in the Hebrew Bible to identify a particular set of historical circumstances, physical and material in content, where the 'stuffness' of creation is celebrated in earthy enjoyment or lamented in pain and suffering. The fabric of everyday living is the context in which God's servants, both individually and corporately, experience God's saving presence.

Salvation, covenant and lovingkindness

From the viewpoint of the Hebrew scriptures there can be little doubt that life itself is life *together.* The life of the individual is made up of a web of relationships with others and with God. Much scholarly ink has been spilt over how and when the idea of covenant entered Jewish thought but there can be no dispute that deeply rooted in the Hebrew psyche is the importance of the family and the kinship group. Everyone belongs to someone else by ties of blood. However, from the perspective of those who edited the canon of Hebrew writings which together form the Christian Old Testament, the covenant which God makes is not just with the Jews. It is something embracing more than the Chosen People. In the beautiful word-pictures of the prophets God's covenant with the Jews is not just for the children of Abraham but also for the sake of the whole human race. It includes as well a vision of harmony with the animal kingdom, between animals which would not usually live together and between animals and human beings. When the future king comes and inaugurates his peaceful reign:

> The wolf shall live with the lamb, the leopard shall lie down with the kid, the calf and the lion and the fatling together, and a little child shall lead them. The cow and the bear shall graze, their young shall lie down together; and the lion shall eat straw like the ox. The nursing child shall play over the hole of the asp, and the weaned child shall put its hand on the adder's den. They shall not hurt or destroy on all my holy mountain; for the earth will be full of the knowledge of the Lord as the waters cover the sea. (Isaiah 11:6–9).

In fact, God's covenant is made with the whole of creation. Consequently the writers of the first stories in the Book of Genesis set the creation of human beings in the context of the creation of the universe itself. Life is something lived

13

in relationship with God and with humankind; but more than that, it is lived in relationship with the whole created order.

Covenant creates community. Therefore when human beings fail to keep God's covenant and decide that they know better than God how his world should work, their relationship with God suffers. Their relationships with each other break down. The essence of sin is that it endangers the harmony which ought to exist between God and his children, between members of the community and between communities. But it also upsets the harmony which ought to exist within the created world. It creates deserts in places which should be fertile. It destroys the very eco-system which is designed to support and enhance life, which is why after the Flood the perpetual covenant that God inaugurates with Noah includes guarantees about the continuance of seed-time and harvest and why the prophetic vision of God's ultimate restoration of his creation includes not just human beings but also the whole created world (see Isaiah 35). Salvation is about the restoration of the whole to that relationship with God which is founded on his loving-kindness.

Although lovingkindness may be predicated of both human beings and God, it is clear that from the human side the covenant can be broken and blessing forfeited. From the side of God, because of God's faithfulness, because of his covenant-loyalty – lovingkindness, faithfulness and covenant-loyalty are all attempts to translate the same Hebrew word *hesed* – the covenant is everlasting. God cannot himself betray his covenant. Faithfulness belongs to his very nature. God's steadfast, constant loyalty and love is the presumption on which covenant is based. When human beings commit themselves to each other in a covenant relationship the arrangement should be founded on mutually accepted duties and responsibilities. There should be reciprocal understanding and help. Unfortunately human agreements are abrogated and relationships broken. Only God ultimately deals with his children loyally and truly, for he is:

> a God merciful and gracious, slow to anger, and abounding in

steadfast love and faithfulness, keeping steadfast love for the thousandth generation, forgiving iniquity and transgression and sin, yet by no means clearing the guilty, but visiting the iniquity of the parents upon the children and the children's children, to the third and the fourth generation. (Exodus 34:6) (See also Psalm 85.)

The covenant is founded on God's faithfulness. Yet this is no blind sentimentality. God treats human wrong-doing with the utmost seriousness. Sin is not ignored. It is forgiven. But because the Hebrew writers have a strong sense of the solidarity of human beings, for good or ill, they recognise that it is often necessary for those who are not the direct cause of discord to live with the consequences of what others have done. Nevertheless, when they have provoked God to anger because of their wilful disobedience of his known will they can still appeal to him.

> Show us your steadfast love, O Lord, and grant us your salvation.
> (Psalm 85:7)

Salvation, righteousness and justice

In common usage righteousness is firmly linked with justice. God cannot himself be other than righteous. He is just in all his dealings. Such knowledge is one source of human confidence in him but it also makes God's children uneasy for they cannot have any corresponding confidence in their own righteousness or rightness. However, underlying the forensic sense of justice which pervades much of the Hebrew scriptures righteousness itself has a more basic meaning, namely the idea of a standard against which other things are measured. Righteousness is the norm according to which human beings should act in their relationship with God, with each other and with their natural environment. When God chooses Abraham for blessing (Genesis 12:1–3) no reason is given for his choice, although in the promise that God makes to Abraham his favourable intentions for the whole world are made clear. People will pray to be blessed as Abraham is blessed. However, in the context of restating his promise that Abraham will be the father of a great and mighty nation in whom all the families of the earth will be blessed (Genesis 18:17–19), God charges him to teach his descendants the way of righteousness and justice, that is, to make them aware that the world works best in fulfilling God's purposes for it. If people live according to God's intention (righteously), than all will be well and blessing will follow. God has called Abraham in order that through the right relationship which he and his descendants enjoy with their God all nations of the earth may know the purpose of God's creation and live according to the Creator's plan. This is not based on divine whim. It flows from who God is. God cannot be other than righteous. He cannot deny his own purposes. His righteousness determines everything he does. Put in another way, God has made everything intentionally. 'God saw everything that he had made, and indeed, it was very good.' (Genesis 1:31) It was well suited to the purposes for which it had been made. Righteousness is that cosmic order which God established at the beginning but which human beings disrupt. They introduce disorder at odds with God's creative purposes. Salvation therefore has to do with bringing order again out of those things which cause chaos and with reaffirming God's intention for those things which he has brought into being. To this end God must always be saving.

Because righteousness is the fabric of the relationship of human beings with God and because it is what makes real community possible, when community and relationships are threatened, justice in a forensic sense is often at issue. It requires a recognition of mutual rights and responsibilities whereby God's abundant provision for the welfare of the community is shared with the poor, the widow and the orphan, as well as for the priests and Levites who have no land on which to grow their own food. 'Common justice', righteousness, the norm on which community is built, requires it.

> Every third year you shall bring out the full tithe of your produce for that year, and store it within your towns; the Levites, because they have no allotment or inheritance with you, as well as the resident aliens, the orphans, and the widows in your towns, may

come and eat their fill so that the Lord your God may bless you in all the work that you undertake. (Deuteronomy 14:28–29)

Recourse to the law should not be necessary. Failure to recognise responsibility for other people within the same community would lead to its disintegration, whereas a society's strength is measured by the quality of its care for those who do not share fully in its privileges. Being blessed by God brings responsibility for one another within the covenant people. The salvation and continuing prosperity of the whole is bound up with ensuring that no one is left without food and adequate provision to meet basic human needs.

Salvation, blessing and peace

It is a truism that the Exodus precedes the occupation and settlement of the land of Canaan. Release from captivity in Babylon precedes the restoration and rebuilding of the city of Jerusalem. The experience of being saved, set free, released or restored comes before any sense of settled development or growth. Chronologically the achievement of potential comes after the achievement of liberty. People set free, on the move, looking for a settled home manage with what they can find en route. They have to search for water. They learn to eat manna and quails. Only when they are in possession of their land do they enjoy milk and honey, that abundance which flows from carefully cultivated fertile earth. Nevertheless there is continuity between the two situations. It is found in their God. The God who saves is also the God who blesses. The link between salvation and blessing is the realisation that it is one and the same God who rescues and sustains the people he has brought into being. He is not only active in the significant event of deliverance, which itself is spread over forty years in the wilderness. He is also with his people to maintain the very fabric of their life in their settled existence in Canaan. It is not the former gods of the land who enable the Hebrew tribes to thrive in their new environment. It is the God who brought them out of Egypt. He who was with them there is with them in their new land. Blessing is descriptive of the way in which God is immanent in everything he has made, giving expression to his desire that his creation should flourish. Blessing is the presence of God with his people, active on their behalf and for their benefit. He is 'with Abraham' (Genesis 26:24), 'with Jacob' (28:15) and 'with Joseph' (39:3). The result is that they prosper and flourish.

> Now the Lord said to Abram, 'Go from your country and your kindred and your father's house to the land that I will show you. I will make you a great nation, and I will bless you, and make your name great, so that you will be a blessing. I will bless those who bless you, and the one who curses you I will curse; and in you all the families of the earth shall be blessed' ... Then the Lord appeared to Abram, and said, 'To your offspring I will give this land.' (Genesis 12:1–3,7a).

Blessing in one strand of the Hebrew scriptures is the promise of many descendants in order that the children of Abraham may be 'a great nation' (Genesis 12:2). They are to be 'as the stars of heaven and as the sand which is on the seashore' (Genesis 22:17) or 'like the dust of the earth' (28:14). They are to enjoy fame and a high reputation (12:2), a position achieved during the reigns of David and Solomon. The people of Israel are to be a source of blessing to other nations (12:3b *et al*) and to individuals such as Abimelech, Laban, Potiphar and indeed the people of the land of Egypt who all share in the overflow of blessing surrounding God's chosen people, for blessing is characteristically superabundant.

It includes the gift of fertile land (Genesis 12:7a) with good soil and abundant rainfall. The earth will yield rich crops and support great flocks and herds just as God gave increase to the sheep and goats of Jacob and Laban. In order to put Canaan under their control the Lord's blessing includes military conquest and victory in battle (Genesis 14; see also 24:60). In the case of the patriarchs blessing is long life, received as a gift. It can be specifically a present as when Jacob sends his gift to Esau in an attempt to restore the relationship between them. Accepting the gift is to accept the relationship, with the implication that they will afterwards live together in peace. Blessing is a relationship with God, a covenant which is offered on the basis of his steadfast love. This covenant is, however, not unconditional, as the Deuteronomic tradition makes clear:

> If you will only obey the Lord your God, by diligently observing all his commandments that I am commanding you this day, the Lord your God will set you high above all the nations of the earth; all these blessings shall come upon you and overtake you, if you obey the Lord your God. (Deuteronomy 28:1–2)

A list of blessings follows.

> But if you do not obey the Lord your God by diligently observing all his commandments and decrees, which I am commanding you today, then all these curses shall come upon you and overtake you. (Deuteronomy 28:15)

A list of curses follows.

A stark choice is presented between the rewards of a life of obedience to God's commandments and the dire consequences that follow from disobedience. But all of this is set for the editors of the Hebrew canon within the context of God's declared will that what he has made should flourish and prosper and grow.

> Then God said, 'Let us make humankind in our image, according to our likeness; and let them have dominion over the fish of the sea, and over the birds of the air, and over the cattle, and over all the wild animals of the earth, and over every creeping thing that creeps upon the earth.' So God created humankind in his image, in the image of God he created them; male and female he created them. God blessed them, and God said to them, 'Be fruitful and multiply, and fill the earth and subdue it; and have dominion over the fish of the sea and over the birds of the air and over every living thing that moves upon the earth.' (Genesis 1:26–28)

Human beings created in God's image are intended to be fruitful and multiply, to fill the earth and subdue it. The gift of fertility and the power of procreation are an endowment, built into the creative processes. God wants his creation to

19

thrive. He has made the right conditions for that to happen but within a covenant framework (cf. Genesis 9:1–17). The blessing God utters over his world is a potential within creation which points to the end-time when all will be whole and complete, which is what *shalom*, peace, is all about.

Like blessing, peace is God's gift. It is not just the absence of war, although it embraces safety and security. Wherever this peace is disturbed it is usually a question of repairing human community or restoring a right relationship with God. Salvation may well consist in being delivered from one's enemies. Whilst in some parts of the Hebrew Bible there is a tendency to spiritualise the concept of peace, in the vast majority of cases where peace is described, it has a specific historical orientation and is solidly material and physical in content. Salvation, blessing and peace are all conceived in terms of a concrete and tangible prosperity, with abundant crops, fertile soil, a plentiful water-supply, long life, well-being and freedom, including freedom from war.

> . . . the Lord your God is bringing you into a good land, a land with flowing streams, with springs and underground waters welling up in valleys and hills, a land of wheat and barley, of vines and fig trees and pomegranates, a land of olive trees and honey, a land where you may eat bread without scarcity, where you will lack nothing, a land whose stones are iron and from whose hills you may mine copper. You shall eat your fill and bless the Lord your God for the good land that he has given you. (Deuteronomy 8:7–10)

> During Solomon's lifetime Judah and Israel lived in safety, from Dan even to Beersheba, all of them under their vines and fig trees. (1 Kings 4:25)

In his vision of the peace and security that are to be found in obedience to the will of God the prophet sees the nations flocking to Jerusalem to be instructed in the ways of God.

> . . . they shall beat their swords into plowshares, and their spears into pruning hooks; nation shall not lift up sword against nation, neither shall they learn war any more; but they shall sit under their own vines and under their own fig trees, and no one shall

make them afraid; for the mouth of the Lord of hosts has spoken.
(Micah 4:3b–4)

The Hebrew Bible sets before us a picture of peace and
wholeness in graphic physical detail. Salvation is ultimately
known in new creation. The potential for its achievement
God planted within creation at the beginning. However, the
people's confidence that this vision will one day become a
reality rests first and foremost on the nature of the God who
brought them into being and then on the quality of his
dealings with them in the past.

Salvation and remembrance

Salvation may be experienced as deliverance, as release, as
redemption. It may be experienced in ordinary, everyday
affairs such as recovery from an illness, the payment of a
debt, the resolution of a dispute, or being vindicated in the
courts. The shape of the need determines how it is
expressed. However, in the Hebrew Bible the only source of
salvation is God. The Jews learned neither to put their faith
in treaties made between nations nor to seek justification
from any human agency. Only God could save them.

> Yet I have been the Lord your God ever since the land of Egypt;
> you know no God but me, and besides me there is no saviour. It
> was I who fed you in the wilderness, in the land of drought.
> (Hosea 13:4–5)

It is God who will guarantee their future deliverance and
the new creation. He may from time to time send them
people to deliver them in his name from particular crises
but it is God who remains the origin of salvation. In time
there grew up indeed within Israel the expectation of a
future anointed king, a messiah in the line of King David,
but he is consistently 'my servant' (Isaiah 42:1; 52:13). This
is not the Lord God of Israel himself, although this servant is
filled with the spirit of God and is sent by him. God alone
is responsible for the salvation of what he has made.

The assurance that he will go on delivering his people is
based on the way in which he acted towards them in the

past. He made them a nation by setting them free from slavery in Egypt. The salvation which they experienced in the past is made present – and a foreshadowing of the future – by remembering God's great deeds on their behalf. The knowledge that God has already performed mighty acts in redeeming them from their bondage, in sustaining them in the desert and installing them in the land of promise is a factor in the present and the ground of their belief that God will continue to act for their good.

> I will call to mind the deeds of the Lord; I will remember your wonders of old. I will meditate on all your work, and muse on your mighty deeds. (Psalm 77:11–12)

> Remember that you were a slave in Egypt, and diligently observe these statutes. (Deuteronomy 16:12)

However, not only is the nation enjoined to remember what God has done for them, God is also asked constantly to 'remember Abraham, Isaac, and Israel, your servants' (Exodus 32:13ff.) God is asked not to forget his promises in spite of his people's apostasy.

> Lead me in your truth, and teach me, for you are the God of my salvation; for you I wait all day long. Be mindful of your mercy, O Lord, and of your steadfast love, for they have been from of old. Do not remember the sins of my youth or my transgressions; according to your steadfast love remember me, for your goodness' sake, O Lord. (Psalm 25:5–7)

It is the celebration of the feast of the Passover that reminds the people supremely of their deliverance. It is a day of remembrance (Exodus 12:14) in which Jews recall that they were slaves in Egypt, not just that their ancestors were slaves but that they themselves were slaves. The past is made present in their recital of the events and by their active participation in the story, much in the way Christians remember Jesus in the Christian Eucharist. At the same time, the present experience of redemption points forward to the end-time, to that vision of wholeness and peace when everything will be as God intends it. It is above all in worship that God's great deeds are celebrated. In worship he is praised by his children calling to mind what he has done. It is in essence a re-presentation of the facts of their salvation history so that they become a factor in the present, making the covenant ever new.

The Hebrew Bible and followers of the new way

It is extremely difficult for Christians to read the Hebrew Bible without seeing it through Christian spectacles. Because of the designation of it as 'Old' Testament or 'old' covenant it is immediately felt to be something superseded and it becomes hard to read it as a set of documents with their own integrity and capable of development other than the Christian way. It is easy to forget the living tradition of Judaism or to dismiss it as an aberration from the true way. Nevertheless Christians are obliged to take the Old Testament seriously if only because Jesus himself was a Jew and the Hebrew writings were the scriptures he knew. There is manifest discontinuity between the dispensation of the Jews and the dispensation of Jesus the Christ. 'You have heard that it was said ... But I say to you ...' Matthew 5:27–28). Jesus brings new insights. There is, however, also continuity. 'Do not think that I have come to abolish the law or the prophets; I have come not to abolish but to fulfill ...' (Matthew 5:17ff.) In their formal structures the old and the new covenants do not differ. The new element in the covenant is its new historical foundation in Jesus whom Christians acknowledge as the Christ.

The New Testament records do not pretend to be an exhaustive account of everything that Jesus said and did. There may therefore have to be some things which are just assumed because Jesus was a Jew and because the Old Testament was his Bible. What then might Christians learn from the study of the Hebrew scriptures?

A glance at the semantic field within which salvation is proclaimed reveals the interconnectedness, the interdependence, of all life. It belongs to our humanity that we are made for communion with God, with one another and with the world. Each set of relationships has to be cultivated, for we are the sum of our relationships. They make us what we

23

are. A Christian gospel therefore, rooted in the traditions of the Old Testament, will be concerned for our individual and communal relationship with God, for the Hebrew mind knows nothing of the privatised, individualistic religion which is reserved for the home and which sets the spiritual above the compromised world of daily living. Life cannot be separated into the public and the private in this way. True religion will be concerned to promote a social righteousness wherein all have a share in the bounty God has provided, for poverty is a spiritual issue (see, for example, Amos 8). Salvation is concerned with the conditions in which people live in this world as well as with their everlasting well-being. It will actively seek that physical, mental and spiritual health which make life enjoyable here and now. The Hebrew scriptures value the physical and material world and celebrate it in all its concrete reality so that care for the environment which sustains life on this planet must also be a conscious part of our co-operation with God. The whole is intended to flourish. The end is a new creation.

The concreteness of the picture of salvation in the Old Testament should not simply be spiritualised in a way that says that the physical conditions in which we live are irrelevant. Of course, it is possible to place such a reliance on material things, on accumulating possessions that we lose sight of our need of God. Such a danger should not, however, lead us to despise the material world. Riches are given to us in trust and it ought not to take too great an effort of imagination to express that stewardship in terms of caring for the poor, the widow, the orphan and all those who do not share in God's lavish provision for the whole human race. The scale of today's needs would have been beyond the power of the Hebrew prophets to conceive but the principles of justice and mercy which they enunciated, rooted in the Law, are directly applicable to the superabundant provision which God has made for the maintenance of life throughout the world. It was said of the 'generous person' of the Book of Proverbs that in a situation of famine it would be a terrible cynical act to withhold grain, presumably in order to force prices higher, unmoved by human suffering (Proverbs 11:26). An adequate theology of salvation ought to open the doors of today's even bigger barns to feed the hungry, for the enrichment of all.

The basis on which a relationship with God is possible is a recognition of our need and sorrow for the way in which we individually and together refuse the relationship with God for which we were made. Sin, about which the Judaeo-Christian tradition has a great deal to say, is at heart a breach of relationship which separates people from their God. It damages community and spoils the earth. Human beings need to be in a right relationship with God and the repair of the rest will follow. It is, however, true to both Testaments, Old and New, to confess that only God can set things right. Only he can justify. No tinkering with the edges will do: we need a new creation. 'Listen to me, you that pursue righteousness, you that seek the Lord . . .' (Isaiah 51ff.)

Followers of the way and me . . .

It remains to ask whether what has been written thus far is a theoretical exercise or whether it has any personal reference. I am a Christian whose experience of God and his working is mediated through Jesus of Nazareth. I believe him to be the Messiah, God's anointed messenger. Ultimately, if I want to know what God is like, I must look to Jesus Christ. No account of my own Christian experience could be properly expressed without reference to him. He is, I believe, both the supreme revelation of what God is like and at the same time the fullest demonstration of what it means to be human. Following him makes sense of life in a way that contradicts and challenges the accepted standards and behaviour of the world around us. However, in seeking to discover the context and the content of salvation in Old Testament terms, Christian perceptions are often sharpened as the continuities and discontinuities between new and old are explored.

Whereas for many years I lived with a sense of being on the move, on a pilgrimage – an image for which there is good biblical warrant – I was prone to talk of *my personal journey*. It is, of course, important to be able to tell my story. But a close reading of the Hebrew scriptures has made me

25

realise that it is in fact healthier to talk of *our* pilgrimage, for the journey is essentially something undertaken together. Human being or, as it has been called, human becoming is something which happens in the company of others. I am what I am in relation to others. The Jewish feeling for the solidarity of the race brings home to me the importance of recognising the corporate nature of life and consequently reminds me of my duties and responsibilities with regard to the family of which I am a part, with regard to the community and society, indeed to the whole of humanity, in which I am caught up. Salvation is about my personal relationship with God. But not just that. It is about rescuing all human life from darkness and despair. It is about reclaiming the whole created universe from those forces which try to plunge it further back into chaos. It is an enormous task in which we are called to co-operate with God. It could feel completely overwhelming. The magnitude of it could be totally disabling, if it were not for the assurance that it is God's work and that he shares with us in everything he calls us to do.

The legacy of the Jews includes also a feeling for the wholeness and the goodness of life. The Hebrew writers would not have understood the division of areas of life into the sacred and the secular. All life is lived in the presence of God. The salvation he offers is his continuing, enriching presence, so that we experience life in all its riotous profusion as gift and learn to live in a spirit of gratitude. A full account of my own experience of God would have to include a statement about how much I owe to the Christian community, and especially to the Methodist family, both in mediating a sense of the presence of God and giving me opportunities for education, growth and development which it is unlikely that I would ever have enjoyed apart from it. I have been richly blessed in the company of those who seek to follow God's way. So, the key to understanding the unity of the scriptures, both old and new, is, I believe, an awareness that the living God is active throughout the world he has made. Because he lives with human beings in loyalty to his covenant with them, he shares every dimension of their lives. He shares their joys and their sorrows. He cannot, however, look on them in those situations and at those times when they suffer without himself entering into their suffering. He is present with them even there.

> Then the Lord said, 'I have seen the affliction of my people who are in Egypt, and have heard their cry because of their taskmasters; I know their sufferings, and I have come down to deliver them out of the hands of the Egyptians, and to bring them out of that land to a good and broad land, a land flowing with milk and honey...' (Exodus 3:7–8)

He is with them in their suffering, to save them from their oppressors and to prosper them in the land of Canaan. His sharing of their pain and distress is the beginning of its transformation, but this is a line of thought which is not fully developed in the Hebrew scriptures. It has to await the coming of that son of Israel who is Immanuel, God with us in human flesh, whose very name is Saviour.

2 Salvation and the New Testament*

Frances Young

Transformation

The New Testament at its deepest level is about transformation. This is clearest in the reflections of St Paul. 'All of us,' he suggests in 2 Corinthians 3:18, 'are being transformed', using the same word as we find in the gospel narratives for the transfiguration of Jesus (*metamorphoumetha/metamorphōthē*). He describes this transformation as 'from glory to glory'. Whether this means a kind of progression from one degree of glory to another, or whether it is a superlative expression suggesting the impossibility of articulating the transcendent glory into which we are transformed, is hard to say with any certainty. One thing is clear, however: the transformation takes place because we are 'seeing the glory of the Lord as though reflected in a mirror', and being transformed 'into the self-same image' by reflecting it.[1]

Now the image of God, for Paul, is Christ Jesus, the Son of God. Paul identifies Christ with the divine wisdom, the offspring of God through whom God created the world (Proverbs 8:22ff., 1 Corinthians 1:24, 8:6), the 'reflection of God's glory and the exact imprint of God's very being' (as Hebrews 1:3 puts it, echoing the Wisdom of Solomon 7:26). But for Paul, Christ is also the image of God because he is what God intended humanity to be. In 1 Corinthians 11:7 he casually states a presupposition he never questioned: 'man is the image and glory of God', for 'God created humankind [Adam] in his image, in the image of God he created them; male and female he created them' (Genesis 1:27). What Christ is for Paul is renewed humanity, re-created Adam, the means whereby the image and likeness of God is formed anew in those who are baptised into Christ and, whether male or female, take on Christ's name and identity (Galatians 3:27–29).

So 'those whom he foreknew he also predestined to be conformed (*summorphous*) to the image of his Son' (Romans 8:29). Here we find the same basic idea as in 2 Corinthians 3:18. 'All of us' Christian believers are being 'transformed' so as to 'conform' to the 'self-same image'.[2] 'Just as we have borne the image of the man of dust, we will also bear the image of the man of heaven' (1 Corinthians 15:49). In Colossians 3:9–10 we read 'you have stripped off the old self with its practices and clothed yourselves with the new self, which is renewed in knowledge according to the image of its creator'. What Christ has initiated is the renewal and the re-creation of humanity according to God's original purpose.

'In Christ there is new creation', Paul asserts in 2 Corinthians 5:17. In Romans 8 he speaks of the creation waiting with eager longing for its redemption, of the 'whole creation groaning and travailing' in labour pains until now, of the hope 'that the creation itself will be set free from its bondage to decay and will obtain the freedom of the glory of the children of God'. Some think that Paul is speaking still of the transformation of the human creation into God's image and glory, but there are good reasons for thinking that he means the whole created order will be renewed and re-created. This has not yet come about, but he considers 'that the sufferings of this present time are not worth comparing with the glory about to be revealed to us'. Paul would seem to envisage a time of cosmic struggle after which there will be revealed a new heaven and a new earth (as in Revelation 21).

So, as we see, the New Testament at its deepest level is about transformation. That transformation means the forming of Christ, the image and glory of God, in each believer as part of the transformation and renewal of the whole of God's creation.

Salvation

The trouble with the word 'salvation' is that it has come to have such narrow associations. This was reinforced for me recently when I asked a group of students what they thought salvation was. Catholics and Evangelicals alike had been taught that Christ had saved them from their sins so they would go to heaven when they died. Now that may be a perfectly good, even true, statement. But in this day and age the question is whether it has any purchase on anything.

After all, few ordinary people think they are really that bad – 'we're only human', they say. Most people associate sin exclusively with sex, and no longer think there is anything wrong with finding personal fulfilment. It is felt that the repression of natural desires by Christian teaching was obviously a bad thing, as was the generation of inappropriate guilt feelings. As for heaven, most people want to get on with living here and now and are deeply sceptical about what may or may not happen after death. So there is all that to deal with before you even get to the ultimate puzzle for modern people – how on earth could the death of Jesus 2000 years ago have anything to do with us and our sins now?

Current perceptions, then, mean that the language of salvation fails to connect. We have forgotten that salvation is after all an everyday word: that the economy needs salvation from inflation and politicians from banana skins. We have lost sight of the fact that the 'content' of salvation depends on what your predicament is. When Peter finds he cannot walk on water and yells, 'Save me!', he is not concerned about his sins or his ultimate destiny; he is crying 'Help!' and wants a lifebelt or a hand, just like a kid who has fallen into a dirty canal. So to understand salvation means discerning what the human predicament is and what the rescue plan.

Salvation, therefore, means a lot more than one can find out by means of the standard procedure of looking in detail at the word and its use in the New Testament. Although present, with its associates 'Saviour' and 'save', you could say that the word 'salvation' is used surprisingly rarely in the

New Testament given the status it has acquired in later Christian parlance, and often it is used in an everyday sense rather than in any special 'theological' way. It can mean rescue from gaol, from illness, from death, from catastrophe – even from hanging on the cross! 'Save yourself' cry the bystanders as they watch Jesus hanging there: in other words, 'Get down and walk away, why don't you?'; 'He saved others; himself he cannot save!' (Matthew 27:42).

When the word is found in contexts that seem less 'everyday', it frequently refers to salvation from the end of the world, from the wrath and judgement and destruction that is to come. 'The one who endures to the end will be saved' (Mark 13:13). In other words, it belongs to the future; it is a matter of hope: 'We will be saved from the wrath through him' (Romans 5:9). In the Pastoral Epistles (1 and 2 Timothy and Titus)[3] the Saviour Christ is to bring 'salvation' (*sōtēria*) from God 'our Saviour' at his appearance (*epiphaneia*), just as the 'divine' Emperor was expected to bring 'salvation' (in other words, safety, law and order, peace and prosperity), together with blessings from the gods, at the time of his 'epiphany' or visitation to a particular city or province. (*Parousia*, 'presence' or visitation, is a word used elsewhere in the New Testament for the return of Christ at his Second Coming.) Contemporary political language is parodied to show that Christians have another allegiance; they are citizens of God's Empire, not Caesar's, and in the end they will have salvation at the 'epiphany' of the king designated by God. Salvation from sin is part of the process of preparation for that great event, for those who are to survive the final cataclysm are the ones chosen, purified and made holy as the loyal and perfected servants of God's Messiah.

In the modern context, many have chosen to speak of 'liberation' rather than 'salvation'. This is justifiable on the grounds that to 'rescue' or 'save' someone from something is often to 'free' them from whatever it is, and the New Testament itself uses the language of freedom alongside that of salvation. To speak of liberation is to exploit contemporary political language as the Pastoral Epistles exploited Roman imperial terms in speaking of 'salvation'. But the language of liberation and salvation tends to become limited

31

by whatever 'shackles' people want to get rid of. It is notoriously difficult to state positively what 'freedom' is, and in fact human beings always have to accept constraints: it is simply impossible for each individual, or indeed each ethnic group, to do or to possess everything they like or want. 'Others' have to accommodated; you cannot have rights without duties and obligations. What we need, surely, is more than the removal of what seems to bind us.

We have become very conscious that the world is a mess and that much of that mess is the result of human failure. Do we not need human transformation, a transformation of individuals and of society? Could it not be that 'transformation', as outlined earlier, might release the notion of salvation from its narrowness and enable us to grasp more fully what the New Testament is about?

The transforming story

The New Testament cannot be understood in isolation from the rest of the Bible. What the Bible as a whole does is to tell a story that begins at the beginning and ends at the end. It invites us to see ourselves as participating in that story, for 'the end is not yet'.

Human identities are formed by stories; who we are derives from our sense of where we came from and where we are going to, by a feeling for our past and our future. Many people in our culture associate stories with childhood and 'truth' with 'facts'. But this is to blind ourselves to the omnipresence of narratives in our lives. We all shape our lives by turning our experiences – even incidents in the office or on the tube-train – into stories that we tell to one another, revealing much about ourselves in the various versions we produce. For we only notice what seems significant, and memory immediately selects and shapes. There are, of course, happenings and 'facts' involved, but distinguishing these from the interpretative account is not so straightforward as used to be assumed. 'Post-modernism' has challenged the confidence of modernity that 'fact' and 'interpretation' can be distinguished.

So we live a 'story-shaped' existence and we have no direct

access to 'experience' apart from the stories we tell about it. We model our own story-telling on stories we have been told. As individuals we 'construct' our autobiography by hindsight,[4] tracing not just sequence but cause and effect, climax, resolution, tragedy. As nations we 'shape' our history, making arbitrary events seem meaningful because of what they later led up to. If we want to know why one church is different from another we refer to the story of how the separation came about, and there will be different versions with different emphases told from different standpoints. The 'telling' of 'our' story establishes our identity.

This process of story-shaping is even more important in relation to human endeavours to understand life, the universe and everything. The Greek word *mythos* meant simply 'story', and in technical usage in English, 'myth' refers to those stories people tell as a way of grasping what life is all about. In that sense the Bible presents us with the great 'myth' that makes sense of our lives, from the beginning of all things to the end of all things, from Genesis to Revelation. All religion is 'myth' in that sense, and to say that is not to suggest that all religion is untrue. What it does mean, however, is that the significance of the story lies in its overarching structure, that there will be elements in it which will transcend any possibility of demonstration by the usual methods of historical 'proof', and that the key to its 'truth' will be the extent to which it makes sense of life as we know it. In the end, the Bible is confirmed not by archaeology but by life-experience.

The Canon of Scripture was formed by the Christian Church in the second to the fourth centuries. The 'New Testament' story, which had of course brought the Church into existence, affected the way the other books were read. Christians had taken over the ancient books of the Jewish people and invested them with a new meaning and interpretation in which they became the 'Old Testament'. This very collection and arrangement of the books reflected the overarching story to which it was believed the biblical books bore witness. So the books are ordered differently, and the story they tell is understood differently, in the two communities which hold in respect as God's Word the Law, the Prophets and certain other writings (what Jews call the Tanach). To understand the New Testament one has to discern its relationship to what Christians called the Old Testament. This means understanding the implied story that provides the overall structure.

This section will concentrate on the transformation story as seen by the Church which formed the Bible, that is, the Church of the period from the second to the fourth centuries.[5] Modern people will undoubtedly find it a strange, perhaps implausible, story – to that problem we will turn later. First we must understand that the over-arching story went more or less like this:

> In the beginning, God created all things and put on the earth an image and likeness of the divine self to act as the royal shepherd of all creation, tending it and governing it benevolently.[6] This creature was the link between heaven and earth, belonging to the created order and yet transcending it; both ape and angel, we might want to say now that the controversy over Darwin is behind us.[7] Unfortunately this human creature failed to fulfil its role. Through disobedience and the desire to acquire divine knowledge, wisdom and immortality, through jealousy and ambition, humankind fell from grace and the whole creation was spoiled: Adam and Eve, Cain and Abel, the Tower of Babel – each particular story tells the same story with a different twist. The divine mission thereafter was to save humanity from the chaos-waters (Noah), to restore the lost perfection, to re-create humanity in the divine image.
>
> So, according to the Christian reading, the Bible tells over and over again the story of fall and restoration. God called Abraham and formed a special people, but they were enslaved in Egypt. God sent Moses, saved them and settled them in the promised land. There they failed to keep the covenant. God sent the prophets, but still the nation is smashed and sent into exile. The people return and are restored again, but the story repeats itself. Unfortunately Christians have all too easily fallen into anti-Jewish polemic, but within the over-arching Christian story what it is meant to highlight is universal – the way in which human nature is 'corrupted' and heading for annihilation. There is no way in which humanity can save itself from this situation. Yet it is God's

plan to rescue at least a remnant, to re-create the world according to the original divine intention.

What is found in the 'Old Testament' in promise and expectation is fulfilled in the 'New Testament'. Although the end is not yet, God 're-creates' humanity in Jesus Christ and prepares in his body, the Church, a remnant that will survive the final catastrophe towards which the earth is heading. The new creation is anticipated in Christ. The Spirit of Jesus transforms human beings, and in baptism believers transfer from the old corrupted order to the 'embryo' or 'nucleus' of God's kingdom on earth. This is not yet here, but it is on the way. It will come through a great cataclysm in which the creation will groan and travail like a woman in labour[8] to produce the new creation. So Christians now live 'between the times', belonging to a different regime yet at present surviving in a regime hostile to the values of the new order soon to come.

Well, that is a version of the 'over-arching story', told in my words but borrowing from some of the countless others who have told it in their words. There have always been variations in the detail of the telling. Often God's opponent, Satan, has played a prominent role in producing the disaster, and had to be overcome for God to rescue humanity from his clutches. Sometimes the telling of the story has gone so far as to suggest that God had tricked the devil into swallowing up Christ in death, but since Christ was life itself, death could not hold him; so the devil was caught, as it were, on a fishhook, and had to allow all humanity to be raised up out of the underworld where they had been trapped. Nothing like that is found in the biblical material, of course, and for many people, it would be seen as an obviously unacceptable mythological development. The point, however, is this: the story is always one of fall and redemption. It is the story of 'everyman' and the story of the human race. The incarnation is the restoration of God's image to a race which lost it through its own fault. Salvation, then, is God's rescue-operation. Because of the human predicament, however, it signifies more than mere rescue: it becomes essentially re-creation, the restoration of a wholeness which involves transformation into 'Christs', into bearers of the divine image.

The story has not yet, of course, reached its end. But the story of Jesus Christ anticipates the end. The culmination of the story is a huge cosmic struggle, the disasters outlined in Mark 13, the wrath and judgement that Paul thought had been unleashed on the world when he wrote Romans 1, the victory over evil contemplated through the development of one problematic symbol or vision after another in the Book of Revelation, the wars and rumours of wars, plagues and portents, persecutions and martyrdoms which represent the birth-pangs of the new creation. But Christ, through his death and resurrection, has passed through the judgement, has pioneered the way to eternal life in God's kingdom.

So by dying and rising with Christ in baptism, believers anticipate that new creation, receive a 'down payment' of the divine Spirit, have a foretaste of the heavenly banquet in the Eucharist. But they also become Christ's body on earth and therefore those who have to take up the struggle, perhaps like Christ facing suffering and death. For though the story has not yet reached its end, Christians become part of it. They can understand their own lives, even shape their own lives, by being drawn into the story, committing themselves to be part of the struggle, with the guarantee that in the last analysis there is nothing that can separate them from the love of Christ:

> For I am convinced that neither death, nor life, nor angels, nor rulers, nor things present, nor things to come, nor powers, nor height, nor depth, nor anything else in all creation, will be able to separate us from the love of God in Christ Jesus our Lord.
> (Romans 8:38–9)

There are also 'sub-plots' in the story which are extremely important. Redemption in Christ is prefigured in the escape from Pharaoh, baptism in the crossing of the Red Sea. The covenant with ancient Israel is fulfilled in the new covenant, predicted by Jeremiah, realised in Christ. Everything in the New Testament came to be similarly traced in prophetic symbol in the Old, so that the sub-plots demonstrated the providential activity of God preparing the way for the great redemption and transformation to come. The gospel stories are shaped by their authors to reflect that fulfilment, and half their meaning is lost if we do not discern the importance of that shaping for giving meaning to the story that is told.

This over-arching story provided a way of reading the Bible as a whole and making some kind of sense of it. It emerged alongside the process of determining which books belonged to it. But it does not, of course, do justice to all the different kinds of material in the Bible, nor will you find the whole story in every book. It provides the key to the New Testament in the sense that it was in the light of this narrative perspective that the compilers understood what they were doing. As already hinted, there is a good deal in the New Testament texts themselves to indicate that this is not an inappropriate reading.

But is it any more a plausible story? Can anyone now enter into this story and find their identity in it?

The story 'deconstructed'

The last few centuries have seen Christians progressively on the retreat as elements in the story have apparently been 'disproved' by science or historical research. The trouble is that giving up one bit affects the meaning of every other bit, so that the piecemeal erosion eventually undermines the whole.[9] This is why fundamentalist defence of the 'literal' truth of the whole story has such power.

Take, for example, the story of the 'virgin birth', as it is popularly known (the Bible claims only 'virginal conception'). Understandably, as an isolated 'miracle' it attracts scepticism. In the first place it seems no better than a pagan myth, like the story of Heracles being produced by the impregnation of a woman by the god Zeus. But in the modern context, it is even worse: it appears to undercut the full humanity of Jesus, a doctrine deeply written in scripture and creed alongside his full divinity, for we now know that it takes the contribution of genes from both male and female to produce a human baby. Small wonder that many 'liberal' Christians note that 'virgin' could mean only 'young woman', that there is an inconsistency between the supposed miraculous conception and the genealogy through Joseph, and that in Jewish thought of the time it was accepted that three were required to produce a child – the mother, the father, and 'the Holy One, blessed be he!' The role of the Holy Spirit need not exclude that of Joseph, they deduce.

But what they fail to notice is that the whole discussion is wide of the mark. What may or may not have happened is not the focus of attention in the texts. It is the 'sign-character' of the birth of this special child of God which is the important feature of the way the story is told. The 'sign' points to the meaning it carries in the 'over-arching story'.

The story-tellers are interested only in: (1) the fulfilment of prophecy (Matthew); and (2) the new creation (Luke) – this is signalled by the fact that the Holy Spirit 'hovers over' Mary (Luke 1:35) as the Spirit 'hovered over' the chaos-waters in Genesis 1:2. Most miraculous births in scripture happen to women barren or beyond the age of child-bearing – Sarah, Hannah, Elizabeth. This miraculous birth happens to a pre-menstrual girl. It is a fresh act of creation within the stuff of human life. Its significance lies in the fact that 'in Christ there is new creation'. The story coheres with the larger story, and this meaning is indispensable to the meaning of the whole.

And so too with the stories of creation, of Adam's fall, and of the final judgement. Neither Christ nor salvation makes any sense except within this universal, all-encompassing story. Yet even more than the virgin birth, the stories of the beginning and end of the world have been subject to 'deconstruction' by scientific progress. It is taken for granted by most people that we now know that the earth is round, that it is not the centre of the universe, and the universe is so vast that particular concern for a creature which descended from apes, and whose population has got out of control, is implausibly attributed to its Creator, who is in any case unlikely to exist. Maybe we human beings will ourselves being about apocalypse, but that would not be the end of the world envisaged in the Christian 'myth'. Indeed for most people the story increasingly looks like a myth in the now common sense of the word; in other words, the popular assumption is that there can be no truth in it!

Vision and hope

The story is a coherent whole and finds its meaning only as a coherent whole. But it is part universal story, part particular story. It is Jesus Christ who focuses the story, deepens it, sharpens it. Yet it is the story of 'everyman', a story that rings true to life. It is therefore both 'myth' in the sense of a transcendent, unverifiable story that works in symbols and gives meaning to existence, and history in the sense that the 'myth' has intersected with actual existence on this earth at a particular time in a particular place. It is my contention that what the New Testament texts did, in reflecting on the significance of Christ, was to stimulate a deeper discernment of the human predicament,[10] and so produce a new reading of the Hebrew scriptures which in turn stimulated the characteristic 'fall and redemption' pattern of the Christian understanding of human existence.

The core passion-story is a drama that is an only too believable representation of reality, exposing the deep 'flaw' in human being. The hero, presented to us as one who challenges the uneasy *status quo* and the vested interests, both political and religious, of his time, as one who releases ordinary people from their sorrows, sins and sufferings and offers a simpler but single-minded life-style based on love of God and neighbour – this innocent 'prophet' is judicially disposed of by the structures and powers of the day. People flock after him, then turn against him. His close followers protest loyalty and fail him. He is progressively isolated, as the disciples sleep in the garden, the betraying friend kisses him, the right-hand man denies him, and finally he cries out, 'My God, my God, why have you forsaken me?' (Mark 15:34). The details are particular, but the tragedy is perennial.

As we near the end of this terrible century, with Holocaust and Hiroshima haunting our memories, and newspapers full of the latest outbreaks of ethnic cleansing and terrible miscarriages of justice because the public needed scape-goats, can anyone retain illusions about the inherent decency of humanity? What have we moderns done with our wonderful 'autonomy'? Individuals get caught up in things way beyond their will or imagining. They wash their hands of responsibility. The death of Christ is a paradigm story, exposing and judging the sinfulness in which we are all implicated. The underlying notion that humankind is 'fallen' rings true to reality. Great ideals collapse, attempts to build a better world turn sour. Morality becomes self-righteousness, charity patronising do-goodery; ideology oppresses and power corrupts. The innocent are the victims. Nuclear armaments and the ecological crisis confirm the suspicion that human knowledge, wisdom or achievement, carries with it the serpent's sting, and maybe we have now finally lost faith in 'progress'. Sin is not a question simply of individual misdeeds, the little things that shame us into the guilt that hides or confesses, but of massive corporate failure, falling short of God's glory.

However, this tragic story, grounded in the reality of a particular life actually lived on this earth in the time of Pontius Pilate, is not simply a paradigm of the universal tragedy of human existence; it is also a sign of hope. The vision of resurrection and transformation also rings true in remarkable incidents of grace, saintly lives, communities in which love transcends the natural boundaries of fear and discrimination that we all erect for our own protection. The most wonderful paradox is that it is the weak and foolish, even those, like my eldest son, with profound mental disabilities, who in their helplessness, suffering and love mirror Christ for us and evoke in us the fruits of the Spirit: love, joy, peace, patience, kindness, goodness, faithfulness, gentleness and self-control (Galatians 5:22).

The trouble is that in the world of everyday, 'living and partly living' as T. S. Eliot described it,[11] we are usually blind to the depths, whether of horror and evil, or of love and joy. That is why we fail to discern the relevance and truth of the Christian story. The mere 'factuality' of the story is not what makes it true; nor is it relevant because it provides a political programme or a blueprint for utopia. What makes it real is its significance in revealing to us the depth of our predicament and the promise of transformation.

So the core story points beyond itself. For it reveals the transforming presence of God at the very point where God is 'absent' in the forsakenness of Christ, and demonstrates in a particular life that God accommodates the divine self to the limitations of human existence and language. It also generates the over-arching story. For the reality that everything owes its existence to, and, despite its fallenness, will find its fulfilment in, an eternal love beyond time is narrated within time in the form of a story stretching from the beginning of all things to the end. That narrative is a universal and symbolic story in which we can find our selves and our salvation: for it exposes our need and offers the possibility and hope of transformation both in our present temporal existence and in God's eternity.

3 Salvation and Theology*

Alister E. McGrath

It has often been suggested that academic theology fails to address the issues which concern the Church. The 'Decade of Evangelism' has heightened this perception, by drawing attention to the fact that issues relating to salvation often feature minimally, if they feature at all, on the agenda of faculties of theology. It would be manifestly unfair to generalise in this respect, in that there is considerable variation across such faculties. However, the general impression that is emerging is that academic theology regards the issues thrown up by the Decade as being of peripheral importance to its agenda.

These perceptions of a massive gap between Church and academy are too easily reinforced by perusing the abstracts of the American Academy of Religion, where one encounters suggestions, such as the following, which seem to make depressingly little sense as English prose or as Christian theology:

> Taylor's metaphorical 'body', then, is an (ex)tension of the phallocentric and phallocratic technology of modern theology, now confined to a two-dimensional wordplay indifferent to the cries and joys of a richly signed wor(l)d.[1]

Quite so. Surely, many ask, there must be a more satisfactory way of conceiving the task, calling and responsibilities of the theologian, than that offered by a purely academic theology?

The growing gap between academic theology and the Church has led to much theology focusing on issues which appear to be an utter irrelevance to the life, worship and

* © Alister E. McGrath 1994

mission of the Church. African Christians often complain about the dry and cerebral character of British theology. Timothy Yates notes this point in a perceptive recent essay:

> Much of the liveliest Anglican life exists in Africa south of the Sahara, in Asia and in Latin America. These voices will claim a hearing increasingly in Anglican consultations and may act as a healthy corrective to the Anglicanism of the comparatively settled, wealthy and arid north, arid in the view of many of these communities because of what is perceived as an over-intellectualized theological tradition and a weakened spirituality.[2]

In part, this is due to the failure of English academic theology to relate to issues which concern the Church. In his careful and respected study of the history of English Christianity during the present century, Adrian Hastings notes the importance of this point in evaluating the weakness of much English theology of the last generation, with special reference to the writings of Don Cupitt, John Hick and Dennis Nineham:

> No church can continue for long without a theology possessing a fair measure of internal coherence, one related organically both to the actual religious practice of believers and to certain basic requirements of credibility or utility posited by contemporary society ... By the 1970s the central tradition of English academic theology as taught at Oxford and Cambridge, was hardly fulfilling these needs. There had long been a notable gap between academic theology and what one may call a theology of the pew, but in previous ages there had remained a link between them.[3]

This persuasive historical analysis points to the need for the Church to produce a 'reasoned expression of its faith' which has both relevance and credibility at the parish level. But if academic theologians are not themselves engaged in ministry, it is perhaps inevitable that their theology will become introverted, reflecting the interests of an academic community with its own standards of relevance and importance.

Yet it has not always been like this. Issues which are today treated with what often approaches polite contempt by academic theologians were regarded as of vital importance by

Christian writers of the past. Theologians of the past were prepared to give a direct answer to the age-old question, 'What must I do to be saved?', which many modern theologians would dismiss as pre-modern or having no academic significance. Such issues are still debated today. Indeed, they continue to be of vital importance to the Church, especially in parts of the world in which Christianity is either expanding into new regions, or facing hostility or persecution from rival belief systems. The Church needs all the help it can get from its thinkers.

But the simple and sad fact of life is that these issues are largely debated outside the academy, in local church study groups, in university Bible studies and in seminaries. British theologians often complain that folk read C. S. Lewis, when they ought to be reading them. But this is hardly surprising. Whatever his flaws may be, Lewis dealt with the questions that people were asking, and continue to ask. People want to know how to be saved. And if academic theologians cannot or will not answer their questions in a clearly Christian manner, they will turn elsewhere, disenfranchising the academy by default. Basil Mitchell, formerly Nolloth Professor of the philosophy of religion at Oxford University, recorded his belief, based on ample personal observation that 'often when given the opportunity to explain Christian doctrine and its implications to a potentially receptive audience, theologians have little definite or distinctive to say.'[4]

Personally, I regard this as something of a tragedy. If academic theology has gone off at a tangent, then the Churches have two options. They can invite theologians to turn from their learned contemplations of intratextuality and give a little thought to saving souls, or they can write the academic off as an irrelevance, and get on with the job of doing something themselves. It is worth recalling, in this context, that many of the greatest theologians to have served the Roman Catholic Church in the present century – such as Yves Congar and Hans Urs von Balthasar – never held university appointments. Academic excellence implies neither an exclusively academic context nor pastoral irrelevance.[5]

The Decade brings together a number of themes of major

importance to academic theology, and offers a natural opportunity for academic theology to prove its relevance to a Church which is increasingly sceptical of the relevance of academic theology to its tasks and responsibilities. In this chapter I propose to identify and explore three areas of major importance to the Decade, where theological reflection can bring an enhanced understanding to the task of evangelism and the particular role which the churches have to play. These are:

- the nature of the Church;
- the relation of theology and apologetics;
- the nature of salvation.

The nature of the Church

What is the Church there for? There has been surprisingly little creative thinking within British theology on the nature of the Church.[6] Traditionally, most mainline British understandings of the nature of the Church have been grounded on the presumption that the Church is situated within a largely settled Christian context, and is thus primarily concerned with pastoral care and teaching. The dominance of this model within the western tradition can be seen in the written form of the Chinese and Japanese term for 'church', which have the natural meaning of 'a teaching organisation', representing the dominant ecclesiology of the nineteenth-century western missionaries. Similarly, the written form of the Chinese term for 'preach' has a strongly didactic and pastoral orientation, having the natural sense of 'to teach the book' (the 'book' in question being the Bible). There is no sense of proclamation, for example, in this understanding of preaching, which corresponds well to the dominant western model of 'church as carer and teacher'. Likewise, the Korean characters for 'church' would have the natural sense of 'a teaching community', just as those for 'preaching' would bear the meaning of 'a teaching discourse'.

This model has been called into question by the rise of multiculturalism in the west. No longer can it be assumed that western society is Christian, requiring merely to be taught and pastored. An 'ecclesiology of retrieval', if I might coin a phrase, is essential, in which we actively seek to recover an essential element of the Christian understanding of the nature and task of the Church, which has been over-looked or suppressed through the rise of Christendom in Europe and elsewhere. The Decade of Evangelism provides a natural stimulus to the kind of ecclesiological reflection which is long overdue. For example, even *On Being the Church* makes no reference to the evangelistic tasks of the Church, or of the implications of this task for the self-understanding of the Church.

Happily, the churches themselves have remedied this deficiency. As an Anglican, I hope that I may be excused for providing an illustration of this from the Church of England. The 1988 Lambeth Conference of bishops from throughout the Anglican Communion, with strong representations from East Africa and South-east Asia, stated explicitly that the primary task of the Church is to be seen as *evangelism* – that is, 'a dynamic missionary emphasis going beyond care and nurture to proclamation and service'.[7] The Conference gave Anglicanism a new sense of direction and purpose through its firm long-term commitment to evangelism throughout the communion. In an increasingly secular age, evangelism is coming to be seen as of decisive importance in reaching out beyond the bounds of the Church, and bringing men and women the good news of Jesus Christ. Once more, the 1988 Lambeth Conference recognised the urgency of this situation and pointed to the important role-models available for the western churches in their more vibrant sister churches in Africa, Asia and Latin America.

> Though there are notable exceptions, the dominant model of the church within the Anglican communion is a pastoral one. Emphasis in all aspects of the church's life tends to be placed upon care and nurture, rather than proclamation and service. The pressing needs of today's world demand that there be a massive shift to a 'mission' orientation throughout the communion ... This is beginning to happen in many parts of Africa, Asia and Latin America.[8]

I should emphasise that this is by no means a distinctively

46

Anglican perspective. The United Methodist Church in the United States is an example of a denomination which has laid down long-term plans for evangelism; the Southern Baptist Convention has seen evangelism as an integral part of its self-understanding for some considerable time, and reaps the dual benefit of numerical expansion and a sense of cohesion and purpose as a result.

Is there not a case for allowing this new interest in evangelism to recover older understandings of the nature and purpose of the Church – understandings that have been forgotten or repressed on account of the settled pastoral situation in which western Christianity has found itself for centuries?

The relation of theology and apologetics

The Decade of Evangelism has given rise to a new interest in apologetics. One of the most important developments recently within Anglicanism has been the establishment of the *Springboard* initiative by the Archbishops of Canterbury and York. This initiative gives a much-needed theological and pastoral direction to the Decade of Evangelism. *Springboard* is headed by Michael Green and Bishop Michael Marshall, two senior figures within English Anglicanism, yet with extensive experience of the North American situation. As the *Springboard* initiative has developed, increasing attention has come to focus on a threefold movement within an overall evangelistic strategy: *apologetics*, leading into *evangelism*, leading into *spirituality*. Apologetics ensures that Christianity is regarded as a credible option in society; evangelism provides an opportunity for individuals to make a personal response to the gospel; spirituality provides new believers with the resources they need to keep going – and keep growing – in the Christian life.

There is a continuing need to take rational trouble to relate Christianity to prevailing cultural trends, and our developing understanding of reality as a whole. This, it must be stressed, does not mean uncritically endorsing or capitulating to these trends, as if Christianity were a bull being led meekly by a ring through its nose in whatever direction

47

culture wanted to take it. The experience of the German churches under Hitler has ruled out that option. Rather, it means seeking to make Christianity credible in terms of whatever values or ideas contemporary culture, in all its diversity, recognises as having authority or weight.

Theological analysis identifies apologetic possibilities. It involves taking the trouble to lodge the realities of the gospel proclamation in the experiential and societal worlds of its intended audiences. It shuns the 'to whom it may concern' approach, which fails to establish the manner in which the gospel relates to the specific needs of its audiences. The sociologist Peter Berger alerts us to the simple fact that people are different, and attempts at globalising the Christian message will inevitably fail. The rise of pluralism, for example, means that there is enormous divergence within western thought on what constitutes 'rationality' or 'the wisdom of the world'. Berger comments thus on the enormous difficulties facing the liberal theological enterprise in a modern western pluralist culture:

> The various efforts by Christians to accommodate to the 'wisdom of the world' in this situation becomes a difficult, frantic and more than a little ridiculous affair. Each time that one has, after an enormous effort, managed to adjust the faith to the prevailing culture, that culture turns around and changes ... Our pluralistic culture forces those who would 'update' Christianity into a state of permanent nervousness. The 'wisdom of the world', which is the standard by which they would modify the religious tradition, varies from one social location to another; what is worse, even in the same locale it keeps on changing, often rapidly.[9]

Berger's sociological analysis makes it clear that some views will be 'the accepted wisdom in one social milieu and utter foolishness in another'. His perceptive comments merit close study:

> *The wisdom of the world today always has a sociological address.* In consequence, every accommodation to it on the part of Christians will be 'relevant' in one very specific social setting (usually determined by class), and 'irrelevant' in another. Christians,

then, who set out to accommodate the faith to the modern world should ask themselves which sector of that world they seek to address. Very probably, whatever *aggiornamento* they come up with will include some, exclude others. And if the *aggiornamento* is undertaken with the cultural élite in mind, then it is important to appreciate that the beliefs of this particular group are the most fickle of all.[10]

It is thus potentially meaningless to talk about 'making Christianity relevant to the modern world'. This implies a theoretical universality to 'the modern world' which is absent in reality. Every attempt to accommodate Christianity to the beliefs of one social grouping proves to make it irrelevant to another. Apologetics must therefore take the trouble to ascertain in what manner the gospel might be attractive to specific groups of people, without making the improper judgement that *this* group of people are 'right', whereas *that* group of people are unsophisticated or irrelevant.[11]

An illustration will make this point clearer. Theological analysis of the 'word of the cross' (1 Corinthians 1:18–25) identifies a number of component elements, each of which presents an especial attraction for specific groups of individuals. This analysis thus allows apologetic possibilities to be identified, and creative and effective preaching to be undertaken on its basis.

1. Images from a Battlefield. Christ has gained a victory over sin, death and evil through his cross and resurrection. Through faith, believers may share in that victory and claim it as their own.

2. Images from a Court of Law. Through his obedience on the cross, Christ has obtained forgiveness and pardon for sinners. Those who are guilty can be washed clean of their sin, and be justified in the sight of God. They are acquitted of punishment, and given the status of being righteous before God.

3. Images from a Relationship. As sinners, we are alienated from God. God was in Christ reconciling the world to

himself, as he makes a new relationship possible and available. Just as an alienated man and woman can draw together again through the process of forgiveness and reconciliation, so we who are far from God can draw close to him through the death of Christ.

4. Images from a Prison. Those who are imprisoned by the oppressive forces of evil, sin and the fear of death can be liberated by the gospel of the cross of Christ. Just as Christ broke free from the prison of death, so believers can, by faith, break free the bonds of sin and come to life in all its fullness.

5. Images from a Hospital. Those who are ill on account of sin can be made whole again through the ministrations of the wounded physician of Calvary. Through his cross and resurrection, Christ is able to bind up our wounds and heal us, restoring us to wholeness and spiritual health.

This theological analysis does not reduce the 'word of the cross' to a single component; that would be reductionism, which is as crude as it is simplistic. Rather, it aims to discern the various ideas and images that are already there in this message, in the knowledge that one or more of these may prove to be of decisive importance to someone who is hearing the gospel for the first time. For example, someone who is terrified by the idea of death could well find the gospel proclamation of Christ's victory over death and its implications for believers as the most liberating thing they have ever heard. And, as Ernest Becker reminds us, western culture (especially in the United States) finds the notion of death unbearable, even if it is not prepared to admit to this openly.[12]

This need for apologetics to be theologically informed naturally leads us on to our final reflections on the nature of salvation itself. The Decade of Evangelism depends upon the Christian conception of salvation being effectively and faithfully proclaimed, in all its fullness. Theological reflection on the fullness of salvation is thus an essential precondition for effective evangelism.

The nature of salvation

The Christian idea of 'salvation' is exceptionally complex and must be distinguished from purely secular ideas. One of the tasks of theology is to provide a critical analysis of the constituent elements of this idea. Different aspects of the Christian understanding of salvation have proved to have especial attraction for different periods of Church history, or specific situations, reflecting the manner in which one aspect of this understanding interlocks with the specifics of the situation it addresses.

Recent studies of the theory of Christian mission have laid considerable emphasis upon the importance of *contextualisation* and the notion of the *receptor-orientation* of the Christian proclamation.[13] In other words, the Christian gospel is recognised to address specific situations and to contextualise the notion of salvation in those situations. To those who are oppressed, whether spiritually or politically, the gospel message is that of liberation. To those who are burdened by the weight of personal guilt, the 'good news' is that of forgiveness and pardon.

The gospel is thus related to the specific situation of its audience – in other words, it is receptor-orientated. If any of the following models of salvation were to be regarded as totally constitutive of the Christian understanding of salvation, a severely truncated and reduced gospel would result. In what follows, we shall explore three components of this understanding, and indicate the situations in which they have particular appeal and relevance. However, it must be appreciated that others are addressed in the course of the remaining contributions to this volume, to which the reader is referred. What follows is a sampling of the outcome of theological analysis, with a brief indication of its relevance for apologetics and evangelism.

1. Deification

'God became man in order that we might become God.' This theological refrain may be discerned as underlying much of the soteriological reflections of the eastern Christian tradition, both during the patristic period and in the modern Greek and Russian Orthodox theological traditions. As the citation suggests, there is an especially strong link between the doctrine of the incarnation and this understanding of salvation. For Athanasius, salvation consists in the human participation in the being of God. The divine Logos is imparted to humanity through the incarnation. On the basis of the assumption of a universal human nature, Athanasius concluded that the Logos did not assume merely the specific human existence of Jesus Christ, but human nature in general. As a consequence, all human beings are able to share in the deification which results from the incarnation. Human nature was created with the object of sharing in the being of God; through the descent of the Logos, this capacity is finally realised.

A distinction must be drawn between the idea of deification as 'becoming God (*theosis*)' and as 'becoming like God (*homoiosis theoi*)'. The first, associated with the Alexandrian school, conceives of deification as a union with the substance of God; the second, associated with the Antiochene school, interprets the believer's relationship with God more in terms of a participation in that which is divine, often conceived in terms of ethical perfection.

The importance of this idea of deification to the Decade of Evangelism will be obvious. For some, this understanding of salvation will be deeply attractive, corresponding to a deep sense of 'longing for God' which can only find its fulfilment through a union with God. Pascal's *Pensées* are a powerful witness to this sense of longing. Pascal was possessed of a profound sense that escape from the world was impossible; that there was no hope in this world of achieving the absolute. The tension in human existence which arises through possessing a vision of the absolute, and yet simultaneously knowing that it is unobtainable in this life, finds its expression in the 'grandeur and misery' of created existence.[14]

2. Righteousness in the sight of God

'How do I find a gracious God?' Martin Luther's question has resonated down the centuries for those who shared his heartfelt conviction that sinners could not hope to find acceptance in the sight of a righteous God.[15] For Luther, the question of salvation came to be linked with the issue of how guilt-ridden humans could ever possess a righteousness which would enable them to stand in God's presence. For Luther, the gospel offered a justifying righteousness to believers – a righteousness which would shield them from condemnation, and permit them to enter into the presence of God.

Such insights were developed within later Protestant orthodoxy and achieved a wide circulation in popular Protestant devotional writings and hymns, especially within early Methodism. In a period in which the threat of divine punishment was taken with considerable seriousness (witness Jonathan Edwards' passionate sermons on this theme), the idea of deliverance from condemnation on account of sin was regarded as of central importance to the gospel. One of the hymns to express this concern for righteousness in the sight of God with particular force is Charles Wesley's 'And can it be?', the last verse of which includes the following lines:

> No condemnation now I dread;
> Jesus, and all in him, is mine!
> Alive in him, my living head,
> And clothed in righteousness divine.

This element of the Christian understanding of salvation continues to be of importance. The notion of 'justification' itself is problematic for many in modern western culture; it is also somewhat difficult to express in Chinese and other far eastern languages, which are becoming of increasing importance to this discussion through the expansion of Christianity in these regions. However, the fundamental concept of *acceptance*, which can be argued to lie behind the notion of justification, is of major importance within western culture, and allows important points of contact with contemporary cultural anxieties.

Paul Tillich's famous restatement of the doctrine of justification by faith – 'accept that you have been accepted, despite being unacceptable' – continues to be helpful, especially for those who have chronically low self-esteem.[16] The knowledge that one has been accepted through faith can be a decisive turning point in the lives of those who feel that they are undervalued or unloved.

3. Authentic human existence

The rise in existentialism brought with it a new concern for authentic human existence. Existentialism, protesting against the dehumanising tendency to treat humans as objects devoid of any subjective existence, demanded that attention be paid to the inner lives of individuals. Martin Heidegger's distinction between 'authentic existence' and 'inauthentic existence' represented an important statement of the bipolar structure of human existence. Two options were open. Rudolf Bultmann, developing such an approach, argued that the New Testament spoke of two possible modes of human existence: an authentic or redeemed existence, characterised by faith in God, and an inauthentic existence, characterised by being fettered to the transient material order. For Bultmann, Christ made possible and available, through the *kerygma*, authentic existence.[17]

Bultmann does not entirely reduce salvation to the notion of 'authentic existence', as if Christianity related solely to the experiential world of individuals. However, the emphasis that he placed upon this notion tended to create the impression that this was the sum total of the 'salvation' offered through the gospel. A related approach was developed by Paul Tillich, using a slightly different set of terms. Within the context of Tillich's system, 'salvation' does indeed seem to be reduced to little more than a general human philosophy of existence, offering insights to those who are aware of tensions within their personal existence. This outlook has been criticised by many concerned with the transcendent elements of salvation, as well as those wishing to draw attention to the political and social aspects of the Christian gospel, such as liberation theology, which is explored in a later chapter.

While recognising the validity of these criticisms, we should not overlook the merits of the existentialist approach. For there are many, especially in western societies, who feel existentially alienated. They may not be sure quite what or whom they are alienated from; yet they are aware of a sense of anxiety, of feeling that all is not what it ought to be. There remains an important point of contact for the gospel proclamation here, which can and must be addressed.

My concern in this section has been to note the need for serious theological reflection on the Christian proclamation of salvation in Christ, with a view to unpacking its contents and establishing its cash value for its potential audiences. It is a task that must be done; I believe that this present volume of essays will go some way towards deepening our understanding of the nature and relevance of the Christian concept of salvation and its impact for the world. It is of the greatest significance that most of the contributors to this volume are church-based, and prepared to address the hard questions thrown up by evangelism and ministry.

Conclusion

Having taught theology for many years now, I have come to a conclusion. It is this. *The true theologian is an evangelist.* I do not mean that all evangelists are theologians. Rather, I mean that anyone who spends time studying God cannot help but want to talk about this to all and sundry. On account of the pressures of the academic environment, 'theology' has come to mean 'the study of theologians'. It ought to mean, and *does* mean, 'the study of God'. As Martin Luther pointed out, the 'proper subject of theology is a God who justifies'.[18] And anyone who is encountered by, and studies, such a God must surely wish to tell others of its joys! It is too late to ask that theology should be about 'good news'?

4 Salvation and Church History: Insights into the Reformation*

John Munsey Turner

A recent ecumenical commission representing Roman Catholics and Anglicans agreed on a definition of salvation. 'The will of God, Father, Son and Holy Spirit, is to reconcile to himself all that he has created and sustains, to set free the creation from its bondage to decay and to draw all humanity into communion with himself . . . Through Christ's life, death and resurrection the mystery of God's love is revealed, we are saved from the powers of evil, sin and death and we receive a share in the life of God. All this is pure unmerited gift. The Spirit of God is poured into the hearts of believers – the spirit of adoption, who makes us sons and daughters of God.'[1] The Church historian has to ask what difference such an offer has made to people, the glory and the scandal of the institutional Church. He or she, too, can be committed both to the profession of the faith and to the profession of presenting as accurate a picture as possible of its consequences.

Reformation studies have changed a good deal since the notable renaissance of Luther and Calvin studies in the 1930s. 'Perhaps the most striking change of the last twenty years has been the decline of interest in the doctrinal disputes of the sixteenth century.'[2] Clearly we dare not dodge what Professor Kent has called 'the unacceptable face of the Church' that followed the schism in western Christianity in the sixteenth century (which led to the emergence of the Protestant Churches, beginning with the Lutheran and Reformed groups). Nevertheless the analysis of contrasting spiritualities might enable us to explore how we can think

* © John Munsey Turner 1994

of salvation in contemporary terms. An 'ecumenism of time' can be enriching and challenging still.

We are all the heirs of both the Middle Ages and the Enlightenment. It is not the case that Martin Luther (1483–1546) was the first of the moderns. We have to take him as he was, a man between God and the devil, as his latest interpreter, the Dutch historian Heiko Oberman, calls him. Nevertheless we can still talk about the Reformation of the Church and new ways of looking at the relationship of God and humanity, even if many of Luther's ideas stem from the thinking of St Augustine, St Bernard of Clairvaux and the so-called 'Via Moderna' of the late Middle Ages which stressed God as the sovereign, personal God who had revealed and displayed his will to redeem humankind.[3]

Let us go back to the year 1515, to the little town of Wittenberg in Saxony. The young Augustinian friar, Martin Luther, was Professor of Theology at the university. Despite all its faults and the need for 'reform in head and members', medieval Christianity was producing religious renewal again.[4] Luther was desperately concerned about salvation: 'If ever a monk could get to heaven by monkish devotion, then I was that monk.' Penances, fastings, prayers, sacraments – he tried them all, as did many of his generation. For him and others like him, there was a growing level of expectancy and yet no peace of mind. The search for salvation, for rest for his 'bruised conscience', was illusive. His mentor, von Staupitz, pushing back to a medieval and Augustinian tradition of a theology of the cross, bade him begin with atonement, with the 'wounds of Christ'. Here is still a matter where Protestant and Catholic are one. I remember as a sixth former being fascinated by Luther's quest and his exploring of Paul's letters. It was the preaching of the cross in an ordinary Methodist church that enabled me to see the heart of the matter and I recall the Good Friday after what was a real conversion experience, when the words of Isaac Watts sung in Malvern parish church (shades of Piers the ploughman!) rang in my soul:

> His dying crimson, like a robe
> Spreads o'er his body on the tree;

57

> Then I am dead to all the globe
> And all the globe is dead to me.   (HP 180)

So Luther was able to read the Psalms and the letters of Paul with a new eye.[5] Theologically, instead of beginning with human striving for God, which he perhaps harshly called a 'theology of glory', the 'modern way' which had influenced his early theology, Luther picked up the other end of the stick and began with God's gracious initiative. God comes to us in grace and love, we respond to his gift in trust and faith. This is the 'theology of the cross'. 'I greatly longed to understand Paul's *Letter to the Romans* and nothing stood in the way but that one expression "the justice of God", because I took it to mean that justice, whereby God is just and deals justly in punishing the unjust . . . I did not love a just and angry God but rather I hated and murmured against him . . . night and day I pondered until I saw the connection between the justice of God and the statement that "the just shall live by his faith". Then I grasped that the justice of God is that righteousness by which through grace and sheer mercy, God justifies us through faith. Therefore I felt myself to be reborn and to have gone through open doors into paradise.' This so-called 'tower experience'[6] was not sudden like those of Paul on the Damascus road or John Wesley on 24th May 1738, yet here was a theological revolution which had an impact as great as that of Copernicus or Kepler in astronomy, though much of Luther's thought is found in Augustine[7] (with some profound differences) and elements of it in medieval thought, often as concerned with humankind's justification as he was. This was clearly true of Gabriel Biel and the Augustinian Gregory of Rimini who wrestled with the problem of human free will. Put in simple terms, Luther saw the depths of human degradation, human being 'curved in' on itself. He has no illusions about human pride[8] but he also points to the height and depths of the freedom of the Christian, despite the constant battle with an omnipresent devil, a feature of Luther often forgotten.[9] The Christian is 'always a sinner, always penitent, always put right with God . . . at the same time right with God and a sinner'. We shall see the drawbacks of this view of salvation later, but its merits are great.

The order of salvation begins with grace – free, undeserved love. Grace is always linked by Luther not with merit of any kind but with faith. Clearly most human relationships are based on merit. Arsenal picks its goalkeeper on merit and he is dropped for lack of it! That is quite proper. Your car breaks down, so you call the AA. The repairer comes, the job is done, and that's it. Again, quite right. Or there's attraction: a man is attracted to a woman because of her appeal to him. The chemistry works. So the world goes round. The relationship of grace is unlike merit or need or appeal in that it is based solely on the outgoing love of God.[10] 'Sinners are lovely because they are loved, they are not loved because they are lovely.' This is the love of the cross. Here for Luther is the very basis of human behaviour. It is an ethic not of law or guilt but an ethic of gratitude. Some modern Protestants find it all hard to realise, as did Luther's contemporaries, but it is surely at the heart of the matter, a key to the scriptures, to our preaching and to our life-style.

If Luther stresses grace – God's freely given love – he also stresses God's gift of faith, of trust. It is a matter of gift and response – 'Gabe und Aufgabe'. 'Faith is a living, daring confidence in God's grace, so sure and certain that one would stake life on it a thousand times. This confidence in God's grace and knowledge of it makes us glad and bold and happy in dealing with God and all his creatures and this is the work of the Holy Spirit in faith. Hence we are ready and glad without compulsion, to do good to everyone, to serve everyone, to suffer everything in love and praise to God who has shown in him this grace.'[11] The thrust is clear. Out of faith comes love. 'Good works do not make a good man but a good man right with God will do good works.' As Oberman puts it, 'Luther horizontalized Christian ethics; he transferred its goal from Heaven to earth. Good works are not required for salvation but crucial for surviving in a threatened world . . . the gift of justification releases man from his greed for rewards and enables the believer to be truly pious "for nothing" – not from fear of punishment and Hell but to the greater glory of God and to the benefit of one's neighbour.'[12]

This is that 'faith working through love', being 'Christ to our neighbour', which gave Luther much more of a sense of Christian growth in love than John Wesley, or those who still seem to blame him or his followers for Hitler, thought to be the case! Yet Wesley added to Luther. He preached 'love formed by faith', holiness flowing out of justification, for holiness implies accepting sinners with a view to making them saints in the fullest sense of the word. By accepting the Wesleyan insistence on *imparted* as well as the Lutheran stress on *imputed* righteousness we have the bedrock of Protestantism: by grace alone, by faith alone and at the heart of it the love of the cross. 'Love to the loveless shown, That they might lovely be.' (HP 173)

Now we must ask three questions. Is Luther's conception of salvation scriptural? Can it be stated in present-day styles? How does it relate to later Catholic and Protestant thinking? We shall highlight the Council of Trent, John Wesley, John Henry Newman and the ARCIC conversations between Anglicans and Roman Catholics. Recent Pauline studies[13] have rejected the classic Protestant picture of Judaism as a works-oriented religion to be compared with late medieval spirituality. Paul's concern is not with his 'bruised conscience' or guilt but with how Gentiles can be part of the people of God. But he also had to wrestle with the Messiahship or blasphemous claim of Jesus and his followers. Crisis enough surely!

John Ziesler has recently shown that Paul propounded his view of justification not to answer the question, 'How can I find a gracious God?' but to answer the more immediate question, 'How can Jews and Gentiles live together in one community?' Nevertheless Paul's concept implies first the priority of God's vindication of his covenant through Christ and the restoration of relationship with himself. It comes close to forgiveness with which it is indeed equated in Romans 4:6–8.[14] This is not as remote from Luther as E. P. Sanders and other recent interpreters appear to think when they affirm that Paul did not have the kind of guilt feelings they attribute to Luther.[15] Ziesler also points to the possibility that when Paul uses righteousness in a verbal sense, i.e. to be made right or just, he is talking in terms of relationships and acceptance by God, but when he is talking of righteousness as a noun he is thinking of moral change in the life of the individual person concerned.[16]

Paul certainly uses three images from his age – the Temple and its sacrifices, the slave market and its transactions, the lay court and its judgements. Is he saying, 'Look, it's like a slave being set free in the market place. My chains fell off – literally – My heart was free!'? Think of a king declaring an amnesty and it is, as Benjamin Drewery puts it, 'the prerogative of a king to declare an amnesty without prejudice to his sovereignty. It is the prerogative of the all-righteous God to restore without prejudice to his awful purity, a lost standing to a corrupt creature.' It is declaring right relationships again. 'The one who is put right by faith shall live.'

If we find Paul a little abstract, look at the story of the waiting father and the two sons (Luke 15:11ff.). The scapegrace son has made a hash of life. He thinks up a speech to persuade his father to take him back as a slave, but his father receives him as a son, though we might anticipate problems when they get tired of cold veal! There is forgiveness, so reconciliation can follow. And the elder brother? He had to learn the same truth, that all is of grace not merit; all was his from the start. There is a parallel in Charles Dickens' *David Copperfield.* 'Little Em'ly' has made a ruin of life with Steerforth. Her uncle scours land and sea to find her.[17] When he tracks her down there is forgiveness and freedom, but Rosa Dartle, the frustrated lover, can only shriek, 'Such people should be whipped to death'. Here is the elder sister – and she takes many forms and is frequently a church member!

It is no longer fashionable to point to an 'evangelical succession' of Paul, Augustine, Luther and John Wesley. Their religious pilgrimages were too dissimilar for the conventional statement that each, like Wesley, had to move from the 'faith of a servant' to the 'faith of a son'. Perhaps it is better to see justification as the anticipation of the last judgement. The end has been anticipated now, that is the kingdom of heaven when we are at one with God is not just

61

a matter of new life after death (though it is clearly that) but new life here and now. Again and again the parables of Jesus show it: the Pharisee and the publican (Luke 18:9ff.); the cleansing of the leper (Mark 1:40ff.); the labourers in the vineyard (Matthew. 20:1–16); and the two debtors (Luke 7:4ff.).

Can we summarise? We begin with the initiative of God; he takes the initiative in Jesus. 'Him who knew no sin, he made to be sin on our behalf' (2 Corinthians 5:21). If the doctrine of justification represents God as starting with human being as it is, dealing with it as it is, then this is the drive of the ministry of Jesus. Many hated him for it. This is not just acceptance, it leads to change. 'Go and sin no more' were the words to the woman taken in adultery, whom they were about to stone until Jesus said, 'Let him that is without sin cast the first stone' (John 8:1–11 mss uncertain). The possible danger in Luther's conception and in modern humanitarianism is to forget the element of moral change.

This initiative of God is seen in terms of grace, which is not some kind of spiritual electricity but love in action. But the grace wants to change humanity; God is not ultimately permissive, so the role of faith is vital. Faith is not far from trust. You trust the maker of a cable car as you swing across an Alpine valley. You trust folk to mend your car and not make it a death trap. A wife trusts her husband. Faith is not believing 'six impossible things before breakfast' nor is it primarily intellectual assent; it is trust. Christian faith is trusting Christ. 'Faith in the Christian vocabulary means sure trust in God through Jesus Christ – a trust which involves the whole man, because it is a total commitment, the truth enshrined in the phrase, "Justified by grace through faith" may be calamitously misconceived. This happens if faith is thought of as a human achievement by which God's forgiveness and favour are earned.'[18] Justification means being in touch with a personal God in Christ and that relationship means eternal life beginning now. The ultimate comes into the penultimate. The person put right by faith can be a 'Christ to his neighbour'.

What of the argument that the Lutheran interpretation can lead to antinomianism – spiritual anarchy? 'If grace abounds and we are still sinners at the same time, put right *and* a sinner, why bother to be moral? Every crook will argue,' said W. H. Auden, 'I like committing crimes, God likes forgiving them, really the world is admirably arranged.' *That* argument was, in different forms, flung at Paul, Luther and Wesley alike. Justification by faith undermines morals! The answer is that if a sinner estranged from God can believe that God is for him or her, the battle against sin is half over. This is the psychological value of Luther's doctrine of justification. Maybe John Betjeman has it when he looks into the Bath teashop:[19]

> Let us not speak, for the love we bear one another –
> Let us hold hands and look.
> She, such a very ordinary woman;
> He, such a thumping crook;
> But both, for a moment, little lower than the angels
> In the teashop's ingle-nook.

We may recall the story of the Frog Prince or Max Beerbohm's tale of Lord George Hell who had a mask to make him attractive to a woman and then found that her love had transformed his face into a thing of beauty.

Not dissimilar is St Catherine of Siena saying to God, 'I am not worthy' and receiving the answer, 'But I am worthy'. The English poet George Herbert, perhaps unconsciously, is along the same lines:[20]

> Love bade me welcome; yet my soul drew back,
> Guilty of dust and sin;
> But quick-ey'd Love, observing me grow slack
> From my first entrance in,
> Drew nearer to me, sweetly questioning
> If I lack'd anything.
>
> 'A guest', I answer'd, 'worthy to be here.'
> Love said, 'You shall be he.'
> 'I the unkind, ungrateful? Ah my dear,
> I cannot look on thee.'
> Love took my hand and smiling did reply,
> 'Who made the eyes but I?'

> 'Truth Lord, but I have marr'd them; let my shame
>> Go where it doth deserve.'
> 'And know you not', says Love, 'who bore the blame?'
>> 'My dear, then I will serve.'
> 'You must sit down', says Love, 'and taste my meat.'
>> So I did sit and eat.

When we see the gracious face of God, the cost of love, we can only wonder. A whole system of ethics and morals can flow from it. If God sets us right, we set others right. If God vindicates us, we vindicate others. Maybe this, after all, is where (despite Sanders) Luther and Paul are at one. In the Epistle to the Romans eleven chapters are about wrath, grace, faith, the place of the Gentiles. Then comes the crucial 'Therefore' – the Christian life-style follows.'Luther is a reminder to Catholic and Protestant alike that the strength of Christianity is its refusal to turn away from the central and unpalatable facts of human self-destructiveness, that it is there, in the bitterest places of alienation, that the depth and scope of Christ's victory can be tasted and the secret joy which transforms all experience from within can come to birth, the hidden but all-pervading liberation.'[21]

Yet did Lutheranism, rejecting the style of spirituality which suggested that the 'religious' could seek 'counsels of perfection' while common or garden Christians would make do with 'evangelical precepts', tend to produce a religion more for the urban sparrow than for the eagles? Later, Pietism, deploring the rather frigid style of the Lutheran state churches, spawned a spirituality of Bible study, small groups, concern for education and mission which also characterised Moravianism and greatly influenced Methodism. Modern styles also take up the old Lutheran emphases. Paul Tillich, a German chaplain in the First World War, who spent most of his academic life in the USA, stresses forgiveness. 'Sometimes at that moment, a wave of light breaks into our darkness and it is as though a voice were saying, "You are accepted, *you are accepted*, accepted by that which is greater than you and the name of which you do not know. Do not ask for the name now; perhaps you will find it later. Do not try to do anything now; perhaps later you will do much. Do not speak for anything, do not perform anything, do not intend anything. *Simply accept the fact that you are accepted.*" ' That is certainly part of the truth though it seems strangely quietist now and exposed to the dangers already indicated, as Tillich's odd lifestyle showed.

Another modern Lutheran was Rudolf Bultmann, the New Testament scholar who was so anxious to preach the cross without the impediments of outmoded world views. Roger Garaudy, a Marxist who espoused Christianity, summarises Bultmann's view of faith. 'Faith frees us by elevating us to the authentic existence by which we love with the freely given love with which God loves us. Man becomes a person only by his decision to go out of himself and answer the summons of love served on him by his neighbour.'[22] This is very much Luther's *Freedom of the Christian.* The person 'put right by faith' really lives authentically by giving herself to her neighbours. A final modern example is the late Gonville ffrench-Beytag, former Dean of Johannesburg.[23] Awaiting trial for opposition to apartheid, he regarded himself as a miracle of grace. 'Salvation I believe is knowing that by myself I am hopeless and helpless and yet if I want to be accepted, God accepts me.' Maybe only in the situation of a man like that does the doctrine which was the foundation of Reformation Christianity come alive again.

A positive aspect of justification by faith is that it can save us from the constant guilt-ridden 'frantic philanthropy' which can be a substitute for genuine gospel. So often Christian thinking about the problems of industry, of economic justice, of racial equality produces only a paralysing sense of guilt or impotence or the blind fanaticism of the crusader who can see no moral issue in the world except the one he or she has chosen to concentrate on. The result is what Luther would have called a preaching of the law. But if we pick up Luther's end of the stick, we begin with people who know only too well their sin and cupidity and the sinfulness in all human institutions, including the Church. Luther's concept of the two kingdoms − the kingdom of God and the earthly kingdom of political reality − can be put in modern terms, as by the English philosopher F.H. Bradley who wrote of the 'realm of grace' and the realm of 'my

station and its duties', which are separate yet intertwined
and both under God's sovereignty. The Christian sees no
hope of utopia, nor does he or she espouse the false idea
that one more little revolution will do the trick and all will be
well. How incredible in the 1990s so much 1970s Christian
political thought seems! Knowing himself or herself to be a
sinner, the Christian goes out as Christ to his or her neighbour with flexibility. Colin Morris, who was a Christian political activist in what is now Zambia and certainly not a
Lutheran in his political style, nevertheless expressed the
political consequences of the doctrine of justification by
faith, which is very much an update of Luther: 'It is justified
man who engages in the struggle for justice, it is rec-
onciled man who seeks to end conflict, it is reborn man who
works to bring to birth a new society.' The Catholic poet
Gerard Manley Hopkins is sometimes strangely Lutheran.
He puts the idea of our being Christ to our neighbour,
Christ working through us, like this:

> ... the just man justices;
> Keeps grace, that keeps all his goings graces
> Acts in God's eye what in God's eye he is –
> Christ. For Christ plays in ten thousand places
> Lovely in limbs and lovely in eyes not his
> To the Father through the features of men's faces.[24]

There is, of course, another side to the whole question,
another way of picking up the stick. If Luther's theology
stems from Augustine as well as scripture and medieval
sources and his own fertile mind, there were other similar
yet contradicting elements in Catholic spirituality parallel
with and arising out of Luther's challenge which we must
not dodge. Protestants too easily conceive the Counter
Reformation[25] as a defensive, totalitarian style of religion
typified by Cardinal Caraffa and the Inquisition. But here is
one of the great positive religious renewals, which was a sign
of new life stemming from deep roots. The whole idea of
salvation was on the agenda of the Catholic Church.
Attempts were made at mediation with the Protestants at
Ratisbon in 1541, when Philip Melanchthon – who was
largely responsible for the Confession of Augsburg (1530) –

and the Catholic Contarini struggled with a way of stressing growth in grace as well as imputed righteousness, but these ended in failure. This was the last real attempt by the Catholic moderates who recognised that the Protestantism represented by Melanchthon was aware of the need to be sanctified as well as to be put right with God. Later, the Council of Trent – not without stormy disagreements – came down on the Lutheran views in 1547 with a heavy hand.

Vital definitions were made in sixteen substantial chapters and thirty-three canons. Luther's views appear to be ruled out – that human beings lack free will, that nothing except faith is needed for justification, that a person once justified cannot sin or fall from grace (*Did* Luther say precisely that?), but the positive definition needs careful consideration. The German historian von Pastor called it a 'masterpiece of theology' formulating with clearness of precision the standards of Catholic truth as distinguished from Pelagian error or Protestantism. Von Pastor summarises the canons, 'Starting from the axiom that neither the heathen by their natural powers, nor the Jews by the Mosaic law are capable of participation i.e. of reaching a state of grace and of adoption as children of God, the decree first of all insists that Christ alone is the salvation of the world through the communication of the merits of his sufferings and that only for those who believe in him and have been born again in him by baptism. In adults justification has its beginnings in the calling of God through prevenient grace without any supernatural merit on the part of man. The latter can resist grace or co-operate with it. In both cases there is the exercise of free will but the co-operation is also conditioned by grace.

'With justification man receives not merely the forgiveness of sins but is also inwardly sanctified. This renewal also is not merely imputed as something adhering to man from without but is a deep inward process fundamentally transforming the soul. Faith, however, is not alone sufficient for justification, it must be accompanied by hope and love and as the Scriptures say faith certainly must work by love since faith without works is dead. Faith working by love in a constant state of grace through the following of the commandments of God and the church results in a continual advance

67

from virtue to virtue. In opposition to the Protestant assertion of an absolute assurance of salvation it was laid down as Catholic doctrine that no one in this life can fathom the secret of his predestination by God and apart from a special revelation, know of a certainty that he is of the number of the elect.'[26]

The crucial thirty-three canons and the vital Chapter 7 with its clearcut Aristotelian argument about the causes of justification may seem poles apart from Luther and even more from John Calvin's order of salvation. In the eighteenth century John Wesley would shuffle the theological pack of cards again and, while disagreeing with the Council's definition of justification, his stress on sanctification in his theology has always formed a link (often not realised) between Roman Catholicism and Methodism at this point. He separated imputed and imparted righteousness. The latter is not pertinent to being accepted by God. The Tridentine thinking, well styled by H. O. Evenett as 'activism in grace', is not far from that 'optimism of grace' which characterised Wesley's Methodism. The opportunity for mission, too, coincided with the theology hammered out by Ignatius Loyola and others in the lands across the Atlantic granted by the Pope to Spanish and Portuguese colonisers. What could be more Lutheran or Wesleyan than this hymn?

> My God I love thee . . .

> Then why O blessed Jesus Christ
> Should I not love thee well?
> Not for the sake of winning heaven
> Nor of escaping hell;

> Not with the hope of gaining aught
> Nor seeking a reward
> But as thyself hast loved me
> O everlasting Lord!   (HP 171)

In the 1930s the American scholar George Croft Cell, who explored the Calvinist element in Wesley said, somewhat confusedly, that Wesley provided 'a synthesis of the Protestant ethic of grace with the Catholic of holiness'. Wesley, in fact, was very near to Luther and Calvin[27] in his doctrine of justification, but stresses the growth in grace through the Holy Spirit and the means of grace – Bible, prayer, sacraments and other 'prudential means' like the class meeting – in a way which owed much to both eastern and Catholic sources.[28]

The Church historian dare not dodge or underestimate the fearful harm done to the European Christian tradition by the Wars of Religion.[29] The Church, said Gordon Rupp, lost its hold tragically both on great traditions of letters, science and human thought and also on the search for justice and liberty. There was ecclesiastical introversion, failure of nerve, failure in compassion. This was the terrible legacy of the European conflicts that followed the Protestant and Catholic Reformations, the most important factor in the making of European unbelief. Here are the roots of the estrangement of masses of modern people from religion. Spirituality became fragmented into the mystics (like William Law), the moralists (like Joseph Butler) and the rationalists in that period of European history which Sir Herbert Butterfield and Paul Hazard saw as so crucial between Bossuet believing and Voltaire disbelieving. This was the price of division, yet in the eighteenth century renewal and revival characterised both Catholics and Protestants in Europe.[30]

For Luther the home, the school, the workshop were all places where God could be glorified; this was one of Luther's great contributions to Christian thought, a perception of sacredness of all human callings, however humble. 'In the early sixteenth century they were bold and truly epoch making departures. Within them lay ideals of family life and social relations which both attracted and moulded the townsman, the professional people, the lesser landowner, the middle orders who were simultaneously laying hold upon the economic, social and intellectual activities of Europe.'[31] In an age of chronic unemployment it needs drastic reminding.

The renewal of the eighteenth century enabled the new, growing urban or semi-urban populations of Europe to search for and find a religion which could give them vocation, purpose and a stake in a religious society when they had no stake in anything else. Nobodies can become somebodies in God's sight. A way of salvation was offered for ordinary laymen and laywomen. Methodism had great appeal to the artisan and the domestic servant. Pietism, or Evangelicalism, used in the widest sense,[32] always carried the danger – pointed out endlessly by high church Anglican and Catholic critics – of overstressing emotion, but the key features were clearly the centrality of the scriptures, the cruciality of the cross (to use P. T. Forsyth's phrase), conversionism, a belief that lives need to be and can be changed, and activism, the expression of the gospel in action – often enough political action, as with William Wilberforce and the 'Clapham Saints' in their battles for the bodies of slaves as well as their souls. There came into this style of preaching of salvation an 'optimism of grace' which Roger Anstey[33] has shown to be characteristic of the Enlightenment and which had a great indirect influence on Evangelicalism. John Wesley's 'Arminianism of the heart' fits in at this point. While solidly reformed in his doctrine of justification, as we have seen, he insisted on the centrality of the new birth, the assurance of that adoption and, in more Catholic vein, the transformation by grace of the reborn sinner. His brother's hymns at times suggest that 'theosis' or deification which is much more characteristic of orthodoxy.

> Made perfect first in love
> And sanctified by grace,
> We shall from earth remove
> And see his glorious face;
> His love shall then be fully showed
> And man shall all be lost in God.   (HP 109)

One of the subsequent tragedies of Church history is the way in which the Wesleyan theology and the theology of the Oxford Movement in the Church of England never really entered into any meaningful dialogue.[34] Newman (who began as an Anglo-Calvinist) and Pusey tended to see Methodism as a sub-species of revivalism, yet in fact Newman's *Lectures on Justification* (1838),[35] written before his break with Anglicanism, are nearer to the Wesleyan emphasis than meets the eye. Unfortunately Newman has the limitation, typical of many Anglicans of his day, of ignorance of Luther in the original. He shares this with the fathers of the Council of Trent and he assumes the very scholastic arguments about cause and effect in the statement about grace in the definitions of that Council. This makes his argument at times very difficult to grasp. But on the main issue Newman is quite clear. 'Christ is acknowledged on all hands to be the sole meritorious cause of our justification . . . all of us are dependent on the uncovenanted mercies of God.' He combines what Luther would have called justification with what Wesley called sanctification with a subtle doctrine of the Holy Spirit as the link. 'Justification comes *through* the sacraments, is received *by* faith, *consists* in God's inward presence and *lives* in obedience.' On justification all agreed on its meritorious cause – the atonement wrought by Christ. The differences, Newman well knew, were over the formal cause – imputed or imparted – and the instrumental cause – baptism or saving faith? 'It seems that whereas Faith on our part fitly corresponds or is a corrective as it is called, to grace on God's part, Sacraments are but the manifestation of grace and good works are but the manifestation of faith; so that whether we say we are justified by faith or by works or by sacrament, all these but mean this one doctrine that we are justified by grace which is given through sacraments, impetrated (i.e. asked for) by faith, manifested in works.' Here indeed is 'faith working through love' (Galatians 5:6), the gift of the indwelling spirit. We might ask whether Newman's 'Second Journey' to creative holiness was more akin to John Wesley and the Wesleyan theologian William Burt Pope than has been supposed.

Our century has seen further reconciliation of views. Hans Küng[36] claimed in an early book that his view of justification was very near to that of Karl Barth. More recently the Catholic–Lutheran and Anglican–Roman Catholic Conversations (ARCIC II) show a remarkable synthesis of views.[37]

Several points we have already made are brought out. The danger in these bland but eirenic statements is in underestimating the cost of the division in the past and presenting a somewhat bloodless picture of what tore men and women apart. It may be true that 'We are agreed that this is not an

71

area where any remaining differences of theological interpretation or ecclesiological emphases either within or
between our communions can justify our continuing separation', but if so why are we still apart? What prevents
common eucharistic life?

The Church historian is bound always to ask – What did
the spirituality of the pioneers like Luther and Wesley do
for 'the sparrows'? What is the attraction? Looking at the
Early Church in his classic book *Conversion*, A. D. Nock
claims that the 'success of Christianity is the success of an
institution which united the sacramentalism and the philosophy of the time. It satisfied the enquiring turn of mind,
the desire for escape from Fate, the desire for security in the
hereafter. Like Stoicism it gave a way of life and made man
at home in the universe but unlike Stoicism it did this for
the ignorant as well as for the lettered, it satisfied also social
needs as it secured men against loneliness. It was not easy;
it made uncompromising demands on those who would
enter and would continue to live in the brotherhood, but
to those who did fail it offered an equally uncompromising
assurance.'[38] At the Reformation likewise the city dwellers
who were swept into the Lutheran and Calvinist reform
found a faith for their times combining new styles of ver-
nacular worship in all stations of society. Some missed the
medieval styles of prayer, penances and symbol, which still
prevailed in the areas renewed or reclaimed by the Catholic
Reformation. The opportunity for 'the eagles' still to soar
in the mystical tradition is a legacy we can now all thankfully
share, even if Kierkegaard's 'knight of faith' is more typical
of Protestantism, the conscientious bureaucrat!

The Evangelical Revival again swept many into the orbit
of faith, even if J. H. Plumb is astute in his claim that
Methodism was more a religion *for* the poor than *of* the
poor.[39] This was not the case with the later Primitive Methodism, pioneered in the Potteries, not by Oxford dons but
by a carpenter and a potter. The way in which Primitive
Methodism produced a self-disciplined, self-respecting, self-
educated, self-reliant person is a story of how religion and
social cohesion and purposeful living can go together.[40] The
liberty given in conversion led to the liberty of the Christian

in politics and social life, as Martin Luther had hoped it would. The dangers of smugness and complacency are clear also. What now?

Are the models of salvation we have outlined too existential and individual? Do contemporary men and women seek a gracious God or a gracious neighbour? With the demise of the devil (in the west!) and the 'abolition' of hell in the more liberal forms of Protestantism, is salvation now something even more existential than in Luther's scheme, with an affinity with psychological concern for self-fulfilment and wholeness? The stress in salvation thinking on justice in the politico-economic sense is needed to redeem this, so long as there is no substitution of political solutions for the need for relationship with God, which transcends all politics. For the Church, Richard Holloway's warning takes us back to Luther. 'Gradually the order of the Gospel is reversed by the institution that claims to enshrine it, and we end not with acceptance leading to holiness but with holiness as the price we pay for acceptance. Perhaps the most gruesome reversal of all is that we end by demanding health as a qualification for entrance into the sanitarium which was established for the sick. And the representatives of the one who came to call the sick end by demanding a clean bill of health from those who would partake of the medicine of salvation'.[41] Luther would surely say, 'Alas, yes' to that and point us to the freedom of the Christian.

Part 2

The Church's Life

5 Salvation and Word and Sacrament*

Michael Richards

'Whoever loses his life for my sake, he will save it' (Luke 9:24). The Christian paradox turns the ultimate disaster into the only means of rescue. Humanly speaking, our instinct for escape drives us to be free of our gaolers, leaving prison for ever behind us. We want to live to fight another day, to recover, to be ourselves again. But Christ does not even allow us to be ourselves; he directs us to death as our way to life. The inescapable is to be our escape. To find God our helper, we must first be helplessly lost.

Word and sacrament are the means by which each one of us in our own place and time makes that switch from death to life. We do not understand this rightly unless we see that word and sacrament do not come to us as two separate realities but as one. They come from Christ the Word made flesh and they unite us with our one and only Saviour. Too often, through making distinctions, we become partisans. We set one theme of the gospel against another. But restoration to health is restoration to wholeness. Salvation has one source. Death according to the flesh divides and dissolves. Life according to the Spirit unites and integrates.

The innocent conjunctions in the title of this chapter can mislead. The first would be better replaced by a preposition: 'through' rather than 'and', to express the fact that we are dealing with a relationship of cause and effect, not a simple juxtaposition. And the second 'and', when it has been used to dissect and classify rather than to join together, has caused immense damage in the life of society. 'Bible and Church', 'Scripture and Tradition', 'Word and Sacrament': when

* © Michael Richards 1994

theologians have chosen one or the other, they have set people, not just ideas, at war with one another.

To counteract the process of division, the Second Vatican Council replaced *et* by *una cum* in its documents. To say 'together with' instead of 'and' certainly reminds us that these are couples that should work together in a unified whole, not parallel pairs that can all too easily fall apart. But starting with and always remembering the unity is the best way. A restored vase is not the same as one that has never been broken.

The world is made by the Word of God. The first word addressed to us is a visible word. Around us, there is something rather than nothing – goodness, harmony and beauty. To know exile, we have first known home. Salvation begins with our learning the language of this world, fitting our minds to its reality so that we can work with the grain instead of against it. It means a realisation that it comes from another who makes himself known to us through the character of what he has made, through our own character, for we are part of his world.

When the Word was made flesh in the person of Jesus, we were able to hear his words as well as see his works. God spoke to us as we speak to one another. But speech did not then take over as the only means of communication. Jesus was recognised as the Son of God because his words and his deeds were one. Deeds matched words and gave them the immediate expression by which they are to be understood. What he taught, that he did. What he commanded, that was done. What he had to do, that he accomplished. The hardest lesson of all – that apparent annihilation is the way to eternal life – he took to himself, dying, not in his bed, but undergoing what we know as the worst fate that we can suffer, a drawn-out death at the hands of our fellow men, turned our tormentors.

Because he believed his own gospel, he was saved. The first of us, he passed from death to life, from the life of creation to the life of resurrection. After his cross, he was made Lord of all; after our own cross, we share with him his kingdom.

He has given us both the theory and the practice of

human life. Because he has shown that a life lived in that way lives eternally, we are given the confidence to follow in his footsteps. And just as he taught by deeds as well as words in his own time and to his first disciples, so also he teaches us in our time by visible as well as audible means, by touch, even by smell and taste, by which we know freshness in the air we breathe and wholesomeness in the food we eat.

Christ reaches us here and now through the words and actions he directed to his own generation. He saves us by assuring us, through what he said and what he did, that we need not hesitate to take the path that he trod. His gestures in their setting are inseparable from the words that he spoke. The pictures they create in our minds transform our thoughts and so inspire our hearts and guide our actions as much as do the lessons he taught by word of mouth.

The fact that he did not write, but 'opened his mouth and taught them, saying . . .' (Matthew 5:2), fits the character of his message. He came to restore the union between God and ourselves; his words had an audience, and with them we hear him. They are not words spoken in a vacuum, but words which had their effect, and that effect speaks to us still of the meaning he came to convey and the authority that won recognition.

Words are not abstract counters, but physical realities that make things and change them. An oral culture exists in the real world in which people communicate with one another face to face. They pledge their word; they trust one another. The courtesies of speech create harmony and understanding. The Word is Sacrament, establishing bonds that hold fast. So it was in the world of the Testaments, Old and New, between God and man; so it is in the people that Christ has gathered together by his words and actions, addressed to us in invitation.

Martin Luther made hearing alone the way to salvation:

> . . . in the new law all these infinite burdens of ceremonies – that is, dangers of sins – have been removed. God now requires neither the feet nor the hands nor any other member except the ears. To this degree, all has been reduced to an easy way of life. For if you ask a Christian what work renders him worthy of the

name Christian, he will not be able to give any answer at all except the hearing of the word of God, that is, faith. Therefore the ears alone are the organs of the Christian person, who is justified and judged a Christian not by the works of any member, but through faith.[1]

But in his struggle to restore living faith, Luther tipped the balance too far. The object of our faith is seen as well as heard. Speech and hearing do indeed provide the key, but visible signs are needed to corroborate the words and, more than that, are inseparably bound up with the words whose objective expression and effect they are.

Christ the Word has established for ever the spoken exchange between God and the people he has made. He did not come to deliver a monologue to listeners who do not reply. The bearing of his words is to be discovered not just from what he said, but from those to whom he chose to speak and from what they said to him. His chosen method of communication with his own and with later generations was not script but speech.

The Word of God is embodied not in a solitary person, but in the great crowd of witnesses who reveal in their own response the message they have heard and come to believe. Without those witnesses, the Word would have been dissipated into empty air. 'The Word grew', we learn from the Acts of the Apostles: the gospel took multiform human shape, in quantity as well as in quality, proving itself by the fruit it bore. However far back one carries the analysis of the New Testament texts, from Pentecost to the Annunciation, it is impossible to find a time when loving obedience to the Word of God – true worship – was not present: when people were not through their active faith made 'mother, sister and brother' to Christ. He showed himself to be the Word by the audience he created and the disciples he commissioned; he showed himself to be the Good Shepherd by the flock he gathered together. Just as 'the Word', because he was heard, establishes his role as Revealer, so his other titles, by the social patterns they evoke, make clear the fact that he came to deliver, not a set of plans, but a work that has begun to grow.

A reflection on the way in which our spoken words find their origin and draw all their power from the Word needs to be complemented by a study of the visible sign-language of scripture – of the context and circumstances of the dialogue. But the first of these two approaches is perhaps the more needed in the present ecumenical context. Having made clear to ourselves the priority of the Word of God over all our actions,[2] we need to become more aware of the manner in which the Word makes himself known to us, engaging our response, remembering that words are more than marks on a page or sounds in the air.

Baptism

Those words that are thought of as sacraments in a special and technical sense all express to the full the strong meaning accorded to divine and human speech in the recorded culture of the people of God. They are words that have their effect, an effect not attributed to human reflection and purpose, but to the saving purpose of God. And all relate us to the central mystery by which we are saved: the mystery of faith, the death and resurrection of Christ.

> Do you not know that all of us who have been baptized into Christ Jesus were baptized into his death? We were buried therefore with him by baptism into death, so that as Christ was raised from the dead by the glory of the Father, we too might walk in newness of life. (Romans 6:3,4)

The words spoken and the water poured at baptism make Christ's death, rather than our own birth, the significant fact of our lives. The people of which we become members is a people that already lives on the far side of death. Christian baptism began with the real plunging into death that Christ had to accomplish. That death changed the content of the word 'baptism'. Speech and the accompanying gesture – carried out as a service even by those who do not understand or believe, but are nevertheless ready to meet human need however it is felt – are God's abiding testimony to the universal scope of his purpose.

81

> In every nation anyone who fears him and does what is right is acceptable to him ... Can anyone forbid water for baptizing these people who have received the Holy Spirit just as we have? (Acts 10:35,47)

The word of welcome into the people of God is the first word spoken of the universal language that is the Word of God. Awareness of one's membership of that people and of the expectations placed upon us makes possible, throughout our lives and at any time in our lives, the denial of self that baptism means and requires. It tells us of the priority of God's gift. It is he who has opened the conversation, and he waits lovingly and patiently for our reply.

Confirmation

Baptism saves us; confirmation commissions us. It is the word spoken publicly that after our rescue sets us on our feet again with a new purpose. There is much discussion of the best age for confirmation, with differing interpretations each selecting different psychological moments as the most appropriate. If one remembers that every sacrament has death and resurrection as its central reality, the decision over the right age for celebrating the sacrament becomes one of pastoral opportunity, not one derived from the nature of the gift. At the conscious level, baptism does not register at first when given in infancy; our awareness of it and our conscious collaboration with it, in joyous response to God's caring, undeserved gift, come later, and are only fully consummated at the end. With confirmation, too, the lesson of one's status and responsibilities is learnt throughout life. The words God speaks to us take time before they are taken in. The gift is given; the thankful response is not compelled.

Marriage

That marriage should be a sacrament arises from its fundamental link with our salvation. Our sin was from the first a quarrel and a separation between a man and a woman, bringing division and conflict into the human identity and unity created at the beginning. The restoration of our nature by the grace of God makes possible an enduring peace in the battle of the sexes. Marriage is more than a contract or an exchange of promises. Just as the Church was born from the wounded side of Christ on the cross, bridegroom and bride made one by the mystery of his death, so husband and wife are reborn as one flesh by the same death. The self-denying concern that each must have for the other is a particular working-out by two people of the life-pattern received at baptism, each day, by the way of the cross to new life. As a sacrament of the new law, marriage is guided by faith, hope and love; a sense of duty, a dogged persistence in keeping one's promises, will not be enough. The old law simply made us aware of our wilfulness and our weakness. The new law is not just an injunction; it is a renewal of our very nature. By the grace of God, husbands and wives are enabled to persevere to the end of their lives; Augustine pointed out that this was living proof of the victory won by the death and resurrection of Christ. The earthly paradise was not brought back; there, they had fallen. The kingdom of heaven is a garden from which there will be no fall.

Psychology and sociology can help us to understand the causes of human conflict and to see some of the remedies. The law can be used to give strength when intentions are weak and temptations threaten. Moralists can teach us to recognise the mutual attraction of men and women as good and to find joy in it through the expression of their love. But marriage as Christ has restored it depends on our knowing more than that. It needs a lucidity born of the wisdom of God so that we can discern our disguises and our evasions, aware that all is not well and that we are none of us without sin. It needs a sacrament to bring healing and forgiveness. And it needs to be lived in its complete reality – as the union of men and women with the God who made them and has pardoned their rejection of his love.

Ministry

That ministry should be sacramental arises out of the service it provides. The apostles knew themselves to be servants of the Word. Among the disciples – and indeed before the greater body of Christ's followers began to grow – they received his teaching and were initiated into its inner meaning. And from the beginning they were associated with the purpose that the message spoken by Christ the Word accomplished so effectively. The Word created community. The crowds took an ordered shape that enabled them to be given hospitality, and the apostles were the stewards and helpers of their assembly. Saving us from isolation and loneliness, Christ was not a single-handed teacher. From the start, he had with him other fishermen. The term he chose and the representatives he chose together show the sense and intention of his words. Prophets, priests and kings had been temporary remedies for Israel's ills, remedies limited in their scope even when they were faithful to their mission. Those who were to be fishermen were given an older and everywhere more familiar image to guide them: for a Word addressed to all, bearers that all could recognise; for a universal language, fulfillers of a universal need.

Sacraments are real conveyors of meaning. They show us beyond doubt that the Word had other audiences in mind. In the case of the apostles and of those through whom they continued their work, the choice and the sending out confirms that the words we hear come truly from the Word, who was known never to fail to carry out his declared purpose, who willed both the end and the means.

An oral culture must have guardians of the spoken words by which it lives. To exist, it demands dialogue. To bring people together, it must have speakers who will watch over its continuing identity. In the case of the gospel, the message proclaimed by one who declared himself to be a servant and who told us to be servants one of another can be passed on only by servants. The right of the apostles, and of the overseers, elders and deacons whom we see taking on their role, to speak for their Master depends entirely on that servant relationship; their status is derived from the one whom they represent. As 'servants of Christ and stewards of the mysteries of God' (1 Corinthians 4:1), they are themselves to be counted among those mysteries, deriving their place in the kingdom of God entirely from God's grace and owing the results they bring about to the power of that same grace.

Their speaking will engender other speakers of the same language. Their creativeness is that of the seed that is the Word of God (Luke 8:11). As well as being fishermen, they are farmers (1 Corinthians 3:5–9), cultivating a harvest that comes from God, and they are stewards, watching over the daily life of the household of God. Above all, they are shepherds, representing the Good Shepherd who laid down his life for his sheep.[3] In the Church which is a people of priests, of worshippers, their distinctive worship is the pastoral care they give to that people. Their service of the Word of God gathers his people together so that all, made one in Christ by their obedience of faith, may offer acceptable worship to the Father (Romans 15:16).

The picture given in the New Testament of those who first held responsibility for the life of the churches lays emphasis on the qualities of character and the experience that are needed for looking after a community and all its problems and stresses the need for holding fast to the teaching that had been received:

> If you put these instructions before the brethren, you will be a good minister of Christ Jesus, nourished on the words of the faith and of the good doctrine which you have followed. (1 Timothy 4:6)

And the dominant image is that of the Shepherd:

> Tend the flock of God that is in your charge, not by constraint but willingly, not for shameful gain but eagerly, not as domineering over those in your charge but being examples to the flock. And when the chief Shepherd is manifested you will obtain the unfading crown of glory. (1 Peter 5:2–5)

The source of their authority to speak, the assured salvation which these shepherds bring and the promise of fruitfulness on which they confidently rely, make their ministry part of the covenanted work of God.

In the day-to-day life of the people of whom they have

pastoral care two remedies bring healing to the wounds of soul and body. They continue to meet the human need that Christ answered for all those who came to ask his help. The curing of the paralytic (Matthew 9:1–8) reveals his power to restore both physical health and the relationship with God which our wilfulness can break.

Reconciliation

Reconciliation can be expressed in a number of ways; the practical discipline of the Church has varied down the centuries as our experience and knowledge of human nature has developed and our realisation of the greatness of God's gift has grown to match the length and breadth of his love. To call the conveying of God's forgiveness a sacrament is to recognise first of all the enormity of sin, involving a severing of relationships, and then the extent of God's readiness, indeed longing, to welcome us back. In a sacrament, God gives his word; however humanly impossible it may seem to us, with him all things are possible and the word that brings peace can confidently be spoken.

Anointing the sick

Anointing the sick with oil is a gesture conveying God's power to heal, the power that led people to believe in Christ as coming from God. He would not be truly represented if his Church did not convey the same gift. But he has not taken away suffering, any more than he has taken away death. What he gives us is the means to make that suffering, as he makes our death, a way to eternal life. The gift is one of strength not to lose faith but to pass through the crisis, whether brief or long drawn out. Like all these special mysteries of his continuing presence among us, there is nothing automatic or magical about it. Miracles do happen, in response to many different ways of expressing our faith. But this sacrament does not make those who celebrate it into miracle workers. They are believers who know that God answers prayer, and they do not specify beforehand what the answer must be.

Eucharist

The mystery that gathers the others into one and for which they exist is the mystery of thanksgiving, the Eucharist. Here we see with supreme richness and clarity how the Word of God delivers to us not abstractions but reality. The Word becomes our food. God gives us, not empty words that leave us unsatisfied, not just theory, however correct, but the wisdom that created the world, the knowledge that feeds our minds, the flesh and blood that we cherish as our very own.

The mouth that speaks is also the mouth that eats and drinks. We take in the words of others and are nourished by them as surely as we are by the food that sustains our physical life. In the tradition of Christian faith, eating the right food is of paramount importance.

> You may eat indeed of all the trees in the garden. Nevertheless of the tree of the knowledge of good and evil you are not to eat, for on the day you eat of it you shall most surely die. (Genesis 2:16–17)

So the story begins; but it ends differently.

> On either side of the river were the trees of life, which bear twelve crops of fruit in a year, one in each month, and the leaves of which are a cure for the pagans. (Ezekiel 47:12; Apocalypse 22:2)

> Then let all who are thirsty come: all who want it may have the water of life, and have it free. (Apocalypse 22:17)

On the way to the garden of paradise, Wisdom invites us to share her banquet:

> Come eat my bread,
> drink the wine I have prepared!
> Leave your folly and you will live;
> Walk in the ways of understanding. (Proverbs 9:5–6)

The use of the language of eating and drinking is not to be taken as a simple metaphor, to be discarded as soon as

87

the meaning has been abstracted from it. A people is made a people of a particular kind, distinct from others, by the food it eats or does not eat. The people of God is defined, as much as other people, by the food by which it is sustained. When Peter had his vision on the rooftop, seeing every kind of animal and hearing the voice that told him to kill and eat, he acquired a new understanding of the work he had been sent to do. 'What God has made clean, you have no right to call profane.' (Acts 10:15).

The universality of the Church was expressed in the absence of taboos over food. The early Christian community 'went as a body to the Temple every day but met in their houses for the breaking of bread; they shared their food gladly and generously' (Acts 2:46). The keynote of joy is sometimes emphasised; but the 'sharing of food' as the expression of the unity created by the eucharist should also be stressed as significant; the social and racial barriers of everyday life are overcome.

To understand the eucharist, one needs to study, not just the offering, the consecration and the communion, but the fact that they are preceded by readings from scripture. Today we are no longer seeing this celebration as two parts – a liturgy of the Word and a second sacramental liturgy – but are realising that we have here a single action of the Word of God, who from beginning to end is active among us. Recent reforms have set about making this one continuous unity more evident and less easy to overlook or to neglect.

The sense of duty or, better, the pressing sense of attraction that leads us to take part in the eucharist is already the voice of the Word calling us to hear and to obey the will of his heavenly Father. The presence of others speaks to us of the Word who drew them together by the same attraction. The greater their variety, of age and condition, of social class, of race or nation, the more eloquently they speak to us of Christ. The readings from the Word of God in scripture place us within the whole historic movement of God's saving purpose. The homily bears personal witness to the message by which our minds and hearts are transformed and makes

Christ's word audible in our own context. All of this is a necessary part of what Christians understand as the sacrifice they offer: the recognition and receiving of the way of obedience to God that his people slowly learnt and that the Son of God practised by his personal consecration to the will of his heavenly Father. It is every moment of that life that was made holy and that makes us holy, not the death alone by which that life was consummated. Christ's sacrifice was an acceptable offering of loving obedience to the Father: a life that was a true act of thanksgiving that acknowledged the source of all our joy.

The profession of our faith is the necessary condition for entering further into the mystery of the Word. The wisdom that has taught us through the memory of his words and deeds now speaks directly to us, offering himself as our food, and we declare what we know to be the meaning of his gift. We give our assent to the Word who feeds us with his life of perfect harmony with the will of God. When he says 'This is My Body. This is My Blood', he is gathering together in one act of self-giving all that God has ever said and done to guide us into his presence and to strengthen us on our way. It is the life that was offered in death that makes up the total sacrifice: a life that includes all those for whom he spoke his saving words.

Here we see most clearly that word and sacrament cannot be distinguished in the Christian dispensation without diminishing both. We are dealing all the time with words that are effective in the world we live in, effective because the maker of the words is the Word who made the world. Words are not just lessons or exhortations, and sacraments are not just ritual gestures that convey meaning in another way.

Further reflection on the material quality of words and the ways in which they enter our minds and shape our lives will bring out the extraordinary appropriateness to the human condition, which it uplifts and enlarges, of the revelation given in Christ. It will also help us to see more clearly the way in which we are here and now enabled to hear the Word of God and keep it. For the spoken gospel was written on human hearts (2 Corinthians 3:2–3). The people whom the Word has gathered round himself and

taught by word of mouth, giving them the salvation of an
ordered beauty of life in his kingdom, are here and now
our teachers. To find what the Word has done for us, it is
their company that we must seek.

6 Salvation and Evangelism*

Michael Green

Salvation is the great central theme of the whole Bible. As T. B. Kilpatrick observed seventy years ago, 'The creed of Israel is, in brief, "Yahweh saves".'[1] And that is even more emphatically the case in the New Testament where 'Saviour', the name much used of God in the Old Testament, is applied time and again to Jesus of Nazareth. From the story of Noah's rescue by God from the perils of the flood, to that graphic description in the Book of Revelation of God's saved people as the Bride of Christ in the heavenly Jerusalem, salvation is the grand central theme of the whole book.

When, therefore, you reflect on how crucial is this concept of salvation to Christianity and the Bible, it is remarkable that so few thoughtful books are devoted to it, and how indisciplined is common Church language about it. When I wrote *The Meaning of Salvation* some years ago the sole standard work on the subject was Ryder Smith's *The Bible Doctrine of Salvation*, first published in 1941.[2] But even he ranges far more widely afield than the actual biblical language about salvation warrants, as well as having a particular psychological position to sustain. Evangelists use the word a good deal, but little attempt seems to be made to discover its biblical usage and therefore its proper use in the Christian community. So some reconsideration of the subject is overdue and is singularly appropriate in a decade which almost all the major denominations in the world are designating as a Decade of Evangelism. Where does salvation fit into an emphasis like this?

I want to introduce some rigour into the discussion, for

* © Michael Green 1994

if we use the term loosely, 'salvation' can come to cover almost everything in the Christian faith. So I propose in the first part of this chapter to summarise the biblical teaching on the subject – dealt with in greater detail in other chapters – then to attempt to answer the question, 'How does this biblical teaching about salvation relate to the Church's commitment to evangelise?'

Salvation in the Old Testament

Several important words are used in the Hebrew. Each has a nuance which should not be missed. Sometimes the word *hayah* is used for what we call salvation. It means primarily to preserve life, and it is something God is pleased to do, often through a human agent. The classic example comes in Genesis (45:7, 50:20) where Joseph spells it out to his brothers: 'God sent me before you to preserve you a posterity on earth and to save your lives by a great deliverance.' And again, 'You thought evil against me but God meant it for good . . . to save much people alive.' It is God who contrives salvation.

The whole *yashah, yeshuah, yeshah* root is the main Old Testament word for salvation, and of course it surfaces in the name accorded to Jesus – Yehoshua – which means 'God to the rescue'. Several emphases become apparent in the widespread use of this word-root. Primarily, salvation is the work of God. To know God at all is to know him as Saviour: the words are synonymous throughout the Old Testament (for example, Hosea 13:4). But this is no vague idea: salvation is specific and historical. It is used time and again for God's rescue of Israel from Egypt or from Babylon (Isaiah 43:16, 19), and this was reflected in all the religious festivals of Israel, as they celebrated, with gratitude, God's intervention to save them from an appalling fate (Exodus 23:15; Deuteronomy 16:12; Leviticus 23:43; Psalms 145:15). That fate is spelled out in a number of ways. Salvation is sometimes seen as deliverance from enemies (1 Samuel 14:23; 2 Samuel 3:18; Psalms 3:7), with or without the agency of human 'saviours' like Jonathan, Gideon and Saul (Judges 6:14, 16; 1 Samuel 9:16). Sometimes it is deliverance from disease (Isaiah 38:20), sometimes from death or an unspecified peril (Psalms 6:4, 5; Deuteronomy 20:4), rarely, but occasionally, it is deliverance from sin and its consequences (Psalms 132:13–18; Isaiah 64:6, 59:15, 16 and 53:1–12). Four key components of this concept are: victory (1 Samuel 14:45), vindication (Psalms 72:4), satisfaction (Psalms 69:35f.) and costliness (Isaiah 43:3ff.). Salvation is rarely seen as merely deliverance *from*; it is often portrayed as deliverance *for* the Lord and his purposes (Zechariah 8:13; Isaiah 49:6). There are conditions, too: distrust in one's own ability to put the situation right (Hosea 5:13–6:3; Isaiah 31:1), and unfailing trust in God's intervention for good (Psalms 55:16, 86:2).

A third word is *go'el*, which means primarily to act the part of the kinsman. It is a family word, and is boldly used of God to describe both his gracious kinship function for his people and also the costliness which that role often involved (Psalms 77:14, 15; Exodus 6:6; Isaiah 41:14, 43:14).

Padah is the fourth word. Its basic meaning is to acquire by giving something in exchange. It is mainly applied to the redemption of a life by the surrender of another life in its stead (for example, Exodus 13:13). It is astonishing that the Old Testament writers ascribed this function to God, open as the word is to all sorts of misunderstanding. The point is that deliverance is never achieved by God waving a magic wand. It is costly to him (cf. 2 Samuel 7:23; Isaiah 35:10).

The final word chosen to express salvation is *kopher*, another word wide open to misunderstanding, for it means a ransom price. Normally it is the price paid so that someone under threat of death can go free (Exodus 21:8ff., Proverbs 21:18). But this is the word used for God's costly rescue of his people: 'I am the Lord your God, the Holy One of Israel, your Saviour: I gave Egypt as your ransom, Ethiopia and Seba in exchange for you ... I have loved you; therefore I will give men for you and people in exchange for your life.' (Isaiah 43:3–4) When the greatest allowance has been made for hyperbole, this speaks of costly deliverance and hints that it costs Almighty God everything.

That is how the OT writers spoke of salvation. The whole concept was very physical and realistic, but it was also imbued with a great hope that this was something God would do in his own time and it would be magnificent. They spoke a great deal of the 'Day of the Lord' when salvation would be complete for the people of God. This is a major theme in the last part of Isaiah: we have no time here to pursue it in detail, but Ryder Smith is right when he says:

> The three great prophets of the sixth century mark the zenith of the O.T. teaching on the subject of salvation. Jeremiah saw that salvation means salvation from the *sinfulness*, and that this demands a change of character; Ezekiel declared that this change would be wrought by the *Spirit* of God; Deutero-Isaiah taught that men may be saved, even from sin, by *vicarious suffering*, if it is willingly borne.[3]

The great emphasis of the Old Testament is that it is God, and God alone, who is Saviour. It is always a case of God to the rescue, whether he uses human agents or not. The salvation he offers is many-sided, involving rescue from perils, suffering, loneliness, defeat, death and so forth. And it is always very costly to God. It is never associated with the cultus: nobody is saved by the OT equivalent of churchgoing, the sacrificial system. And nowhere is it associated with good deeds. That is a very important consideration. For if modern people think of salvation at all in religious terms, it is something they do themselves: they commend themselves to God by their churchgoing and their good deeds. The Old Testament will have none of this. Salvation is the prerogative of God alone.

Salvation in the world of the first century

Among the Jews
Judaism never lost the hope of salvation; indeed, it increased during the centuries after the completion of the Old Testament, years when God's people were subjected to continuous disappointment and oppression. They had to put up with invasion after invasion – Antiochus, Pompey, Herod – followed by direct Roman rule. This was hard to bear. It was not only painful, it was an insult to God whose people they

were. There had been a marvellous deliverance, when the Maccabees had defeated the Seleucids and restored self-government to Israel in the second century BC. And though the respite was short-lived, there was a continuing hope that what God had done once he could do again. The inter-testamental writings are full of it, especially the *Psalms of Solomon* and many parts of the *Testaments of the Twelve Patriarchs*. They were looking for salvation.

The Sadducees looked for it by co-operating with the occupying power. The Pharisees were much more spiritual; they hoped for an 'anointed one' of Davidic stock who would be raised up by God himself and would rescue them not only from the Romans but from sin. This is plain from the *Psalms of Solomon*, a Pharisee document from the first century BC. Israel must possess their souls in patience and await God's time. In the meantime they resorted to a doctrine of merit: 'he that honours his father makes atonement for sins' (Ben Sirach 3:1) or 'the righteous, who have many works laid up with Thee shall receive their reward according to their own deeds' (4 Ezra 8:33ff.). The question, 'Are there few that will be saved?' (Luke 13:23) was much debated in Pharisaic circles. The greater the reliance on a doctrine of merit, the fewer who may hope for deliverance.

The Essenes, who wrote the Dead Sea Scrolls, and pulled out of contemporary Judaism to wait for God's intervention in the wilderness near the Dead Sea, were also fascinated by the theme of salvation. They would keep their noses clean and refrain from political or military action, until the Day of the Lord, when the sons of light would take on the sons of darkness in the final battle.

As for the Zealots, who formed the patriotic reaction against Rome when direct rule was introduced in AD 6, their hunger for salvation was keen and their recipe clear. They would use guerrilla tactics or open battle as the case might be, to oppose by every means they could the Romans who were defiling God's holy land.

There was, therefore, a universal longing for salvation in first-century Judaism; different though the programmes were for the various strands within the nation, the Jews were like a cauldron bubbling with hopes of salvation. It was into this cauldron that Jesus came.

In the Graeco-Roman world

The pagan world, no less than Judaism, was hungry for salvation in the first century AD. The archaeologist W. M. Ramsay takes special note of the vast numbers of inscriptions from this period with prayers *huper soterias*, for salvation. Of course, it meant different things to different people. There were three main expectations.

Many people looked for salvation to come through the emperor. Civil war had been tearing the Roman world apart for a century before Augustus brought it to an end with the Battle of Actium, and thereafter became, in effect, the supreme governor of the Roman Empire. To be sure, his pre-eminence was disguised by deference to ancient republican sentiments, but the reality was clear enough. And the common man appreciated his achievements enormously. They called him *Soter tes oikoumenes*, Saviour of the world, *pontifex maximus*, supreme bridge-builder between men and the gods, *divi filius*, son of god, i.e. the deified Julius Caesar. They hailed his principate as the golden age, the reign of the prince of peace. But increasingly they came to see that, despite the tremendous military and political triumphs of Augustus, 'Caesar can give peace from war, but he cannot give peace from sorrow' – so wrote Epictetus. Where, then, did they look for that deeper salvation for which they longed? State religion had little to offer. The household gods of ancient Rome had lost their appeal, and the new devotion to Rome and Augustus had no power to heal the broken heart. People tended to turn, therefore, in one of two directions, both as a search for salvation.

One was salvation by *cultus*. The most popular were the mystery religions, with their rhythm of birth, maturity, age and death leading into new birth. This touched the hunger of the heart as no external religion ever could. Astrology was also very popular: people sought their destiny – as they still do – in the stars. And magic had an enormous following in the time of Jesus; this was an attempt to exercise power over the demonic forces which control the world by getting to know their name and break their grip.

The other main direction was salvation by *knowledge*. It might be through *gnosis*, a curious form of arcane knowledge; indeed this attraction nearly scuppered the Church in the second century AD, so popular had it become. Alternatively, it might be the higher knowledge of philosophy. These were the two directions in which secular people were looking for rescue and fulfilment in the first century of our era. There was an additional factor. A persistent prophecy, rumour and prediction, recorded in several of the ancient historians of the time, claimed that deliverance would come from the Jewish people.

All these factors combined to turn the eyes of the ancient world towards the east. They were looking for salvation.

Salvation in the teaching of Jesus

There are four main strands in Jesus' teaching about salvation.

First, *salvation is equated with the kingdom of God*. This was the main thrust of Jesus' teaching. God is king and he requires his people to surrender to his sovereignty and to live as a new society. The kingdom is both present, in Jesus and those who follow him, and future, when all the world will acknowledge his rule. The gospels equate salvation with entering the kingdom of God. The kingdom, therefore, was not something you sat and waited for, as the inter-testamental writers had expected. It was something you entered now, and the fullness of its implications would be clear later. The notion of the kingdom had an 'already' side to it, and also a 'not yet'. Mark 10 is a crucial chapter for equating 'entering' or 'receiving' the kingdom of God with 'being saved' and coming to 'follow Jesus'. The conditions for eternal life and entering the kingdom of God are identical – repentance, and commitment to Jesus. That was a phenomenal claim. It was too much for many of Jesus' first-century hearers.

Secondly, *salvation was going to be achieved by the Son of Man*, Jesus' own self-designation. The Son of Man had come to

97

seek and save the lost (Luke 19:10). It was a profound and confusing designation for Jesus to use. On the one hand it denoted the present Son of Man (Mark 2:10, 28), on the other, the future glorious Son of Man predicted by Daniel (Daniel 7:14; Mark 14:62). In between, it signified the suffering Son of Man, whose destiny he saw as interwoven with the Suffering Servant dying for the sins of the people (Mark 10:45).

Thirdly, *salvation centred on the forgiveness of sins.* What had been peripheral in the Old Testament now became central. The Son of Man was going to give his life as a ransom for many. There was no room in God's presence for the self-satisfied, the 'righteous'. His gracious mercy was, however, available to all who admitted that they were sinners, who did not deserve anything from his hand. 'The man who acknowledged that he was a sinner,' wrote Professor Alan Richardson, 'went down to his house justified, rather than the man who boasted of his genuinely good works.'[4] The issue was whether salvation was by human achievement or divine mercy. Jesus was utterly unambiguous on the subject. Nobody could make himself right with God. That was the prerogative of the Son of Man, and it cost him his life.

Finally, *salvation is concerned with the whole person.* The New Testament word for salvation is used of the healings of Jesus: 'to heal' and 'to save' are synonymous in the gospels (Mark 5:34; 10:52; 2:1–12). The deliberate ambivalence of the 'save'/'heal' language is emphatic at the cross of Jesus. Salvation concerns the whole person. In this life it is incomplete; God has a future destiny for those who trust him. And the conditions for entry, as in the Old Testament, are repentance and trust. Nowhere is salvation attributed to human virtue. God remains the Saviour of his people.

Salvation in the teaching of St Paul

It is not possible here to explore the different emphases on salvation proffered by the four evangelists, or the Acts of the Apostles, or the shorter writings of the NT. But the position taken up by St Paul is characteristic of the whole New Testament and it has three great dimensions to it. We might almost designate them the three tenses of salvation – past, present and future.

There is a sense in which *salvation is already achieved*. We have been saved from the doom that our sins merited by the death of Christ upon the cross. Paul is very clear about this. In four places (Romans 8:24; Ephesians 2:5, 8; 2 Timothy 1:9 and Titus 3:5) Paul speaks of salvation as something that has already been achieved. But in each of those instances the tension is preserved between the 'already' and the 'not yet'. What has the Christian been saved from? Paul is clear about that, too. It is from the old aeon of sin, law, wrath and death. (This quartet is extensively examined in Romans 5–8.) It is from the old state, of alienation from God. It is from the old fears, particularly of death and judgement. And it is from the old habits of failing, time after time, to live the way God wants us to. Paul is no less clear about *how* we have been saved. It is supremely by God, by his Son Jesus Christ, by his death and resurrection; and that spells grace, sheer unmerited favour on God's side. On our side, it evokes one reaction and one only – adoring trust or faith.

That is a real and undeniable aspect of the New Testament teaching about salvation. It has been achieved by the 'rescuing' acts of Jesus Christ, through his incarnation, but particularly through his death and resurrection. We have been saved from the doom of our sins and failures because of what he has done for us. He fulfilled the 'costly rescue' which we saw was inherent in the Old Testament understanding of salvation.

But that is far from the whole story. *Salvation is a present experience*. St Paul makes this point in three contexts. It means protection in Christ, power through the Spirit, and preaching to the lost. It can be argued that he ought to have used the term more widely and referred it to Church life, social involvement, other faiths and so forth. The fact remains that he has not. And if we want to arrive at any precise understanding of what the New Testament actually teaches about a term that can easily be rendered infinitely expandable, we would be wise to concentrate on the actual linguistic usage.

How can Paul, with all his experience of hardship, possibly speak of the Christian as secure? Simply because the believer is 'in Christ'. Solidarity with Christ involves all believers in his life. He is the *Lord* Jesus. And just as the husband saves or protects his wife, so Christ saves his people (Ephesians 5:23). In Christ, the Christian is invulnerable until his moment comes to die and meet his Saviour. The demonic powers cannot touch him: they were disarmed by Christ's victory on the cross (Colossians 2:15; Romans 8:38f.). Danger and opposition cannot thwart him; even a rigorous imprisonment can turn out to the furthering of his salvation (Philippians 1:19). God will not scrap what is precious to him; he will not discard what he had saved. He who has begun a good work in the Christian will continue it until the day of Christ (Philippians 1:6). For *now* is the day of salvation (2 Corinthians 6:2).

But the present tense of salvation spells not only security but strength. The cross and the resurrection are a present means of salvation (1 Corinthians 1:18; 15:2). They express not only what he did for us then, but what he wants to do in us now – to enable that dying and rising to life to which our baptism pledged us and which lies at the heart of Christian holiness and victorious living. Salvation in the present tense means living with Christ now (1 Thessalonians 5:10), allowing his Spirit to work in and through us (Philippians 2:12ff.).

Inevitably, therefore, salvation is something that must be proclaimed with all our strength. It leads inexorably to preaching. Paul sees the world as falling clearly into only two categories – those who are being saved and those who are being lost (1 Corinthians 1:18; 2 Corinthians 2:15, 4:3–6; Colossians 1:13; etc.). The Christian has responsibilities to both.

God intends those who are already objects of his saving power to be helped along the way of salvation by the life and words of Christian brethren. Thus Timothy, for example, by taking heed to himself (in meditation, dedication, exhortation and stirring up the gift within him) and to the doctrine (teaching, exhortation and public reading of the scriptures) will further his own salvation and that of his, presumably, Christian hearers (1 Timothy 4:14–16). Similarly, when God saves a man like Paul, it is in order to make him a pattern to those who should hereafter believe (1 Timothy 1:15f.). Not only a Christian's example but his prayers (2 Thessalonians 3:1ff.; Philippians 1:19) can further the salvation of brothers and sisters in Christ. So can suffering, if patiently endured (2 Corinthians 1:6; 2 Timothy 2:10).

But if the Christian who enjoys the power and protection of Christ is in duty bound to give himself in service to – and, if necessary, suffering for – those who are in Christ with him, he is under an even more pressing obligation to those who are without God and without hope in the world (Ephesians 2:12). This became the master passion of Paul's life, 'so that by all means I might save some' (1 Corinthians 9:22; 10:23). It is the task of every Christian to pass on what he himself enjoys to those who lack it. For this is the will of God (1 Timothy 2:3) who is in design the Saviour of all, but in practice the Saviour of those who believe. 'And how shall they believe in him of whom they have not heard? And how shall they hear without a preacher?' (Romans 10:4) This imperative of mission rests upon us all, 'for with the heart man believes unto righteousness, and with the mouth confession is made unto salvation' (Romans 10:10). Only in this way can salvation spread; only thus can God's will for the extension of his saving work in this age be accomplished.

Important though the past and present aspects of salvation are, the vast preponderance of New Testament references locate *salvation in God's future*. 'Our salvation is nearer than when we believed'; 'We have been saved in hope ... of the resurrection'; 'We look for that blessed hope, the glorious appearing of the great God and our Saviour Jesus Christ.' These are some of the ways in which Paul expresses his future hope. Salvation is eschatological through and through. It will not be a point in history but beyond history, not merely its conclusion but its goal. For eschatology has become, with Jesus Christ, a department of Christology. It was through him that we were saved from sin's guilt and doom. It is in him that we are being kept safe from the downward pull of the world, the flesh and the devil. And it is in him that we shall be saved (Romans 5:9) when we are for ever liberated from all the effects of the Fall. It is natural,

101

therefore, that Paul's three main convictions about the after-
life are integrated with the person of Jesus who brings 'God
to the rescue' to us. He is clear that the Christian will share
Christ's presence, his life and his likeness. And that is where
the great weight of New Testament references to salvation
are located. We have the first instalment now, but the full
crop still remains. Nor will it be complete for any until it is
complete for all.

Salvation and evangelism today

That is a cursory summary of what I understand the Bible
to teach on the subject of salvation. In the light of it, we can
go on to address briefly some of the questions related to
evangelism. I shall select ten.

The author of salvation

It is abundantly clear from the teaching of the Bible that
salvation is God's work, and his alone. He may allow us to
share in it with him, but the source is God alone. That is
strongly emphasised in the Old Testament, where God
is constantly portrayed as Saviour, and even more strongly
in the New where he comes in the person of Jesus to achieve
salvation for a lost world. This immediately alerts us to two
important truths. The first is the extent of human need,
since God alone suffices to cope with it. The second is that
no human activity can be the source (though it may be the
channel) of salvation. Salvation is not achieved by the best
offices of the World Council of Churches or the World
Evangelical Alliance. It is not achieved by an integration of
world religions. Nor is it merited by human goodness or
religious observance. It is not something that one person
can do for another: God is the author of salvation. He
invented this rescue for his fallen world. He brought it into
being. By his Spirit he applies it to human hearts, and he
will not give his glory to another. Woe, therefore, to the
moralist who thinks he can engineer salvation. And woe to
the evangelist who thinks he can manipulate people into
salvation. God is the author of salvation, and that is what
delivers evangelism from proselytising.

The community of salvation
The biblical data leave us in no doubt that community is central to salvation. It is not individuals but communities that God saves in the Old Testament. In the New, too, the Saviour comes to make a people for his own possession. Western post-Enlightenment individualism has obscured the societal aspect of salvation and turned it into something so individual that you hear the cry, 'Have you been saved yet? I have.' That is not entirely wrong, because salvation needs to be appropriated by each of us, but its thrust is misleading. We are brought into a community where God is at work remaking people so that the likeness of his Son shines through them corporately as well as individually and so that they become a task-force with an alternative life-style, a foretaste here and now of what God's kingdom might look like. Christianity that doesn't begin with the individual doesn't begin. But Christianity that ends with the individual ends. Salvation is inescapably corporate, as its sacraments so graphically remind us. You are baptised into a community and you eat the communal meal which is an anticipation of the messianic banquet in heaven where all community finds its fulfilment.

The preparation for outreach
If the Church is inevitably a part of its own gospel, what must that Church be like in order to display the attractiveness of its Saviour? Some of the strands that are most evident in churches that are growing throughout the world are remarkably constant in every continent and nation. There is always radiant worship governed by the Lord not the clock. There is always a warmth of love, instead of the introversion of the ghetto. There is always an emphasis on every member ministry: you cannot be a Christian without having a ministry, and the live, attractive church is one where people know what God has called them to do and get on with it in partnership with others differently gifted. There is always a fresh openness to the Holy Spirit, and the expectancy to see him working among them. There is always a heavy stress on prayer. Without that, there is no blessing. How could there be? Evangelism is God's work, and in prayer we admit it and

103

cry to him to act. What is more, growing churches always prepare nurseries for the new births they expect. Nurture Groups, Discovery Groups, or whatever you call them, are a virtual necessity for nurturing new believers. To imagine that they will be able to fit into the entirely different cultural milieu of Church life from day one is sheer fantasy. They need the most careful nurture; they need loving care; they need to be listened to and to have their questions answered. And God does not generally bring much new life into churches that fail to make that provision. He does not put live chicks under dead hens.

The breadth of the concept

If we take the Bible as our guide, salvation is a very broad and deep river that fertilises all it touches. It is like a many-faceted diamond, reflecting God's succour towards peril, pain, frustration, loneliness, guilt, defeat and death. It is nothing less than God's intervention for his people in every detail of their lives, and it culminates in a wonderful reunion in heaven. Any attempt, therefore, to identify salvation with a prayer of commitment uttered at the end of a sermon by an evangelist is grossly to impoverish it. And since salvation is as broad as human need, it should not surprise us that God gets through to different people in very different ways with his good news of salvation. There is nothing mono-chrome about our God – nor should there be about our evangelists!

The content of the message

To say that salvation is as broad as human need must never allow us to hold vague views on it. There is a decisiveness about it. And to this extent the enthusiastic evangelist is right. But the decisiveness comes from God's historic act, not from our instant decision. The distinction is crucial. Something happened in history, in the broken flesh of Jesus on the cross, which enabled God to accept us when in ourselves we were unacceptable. Once, upon that cross, he did for humanity what humanity could never do for itself. He dealt with our alienation and guilt at its root, by taking the consequences upon himself. And because he has saddled himself with our debts, and died our death, there is a glorious decisiveness about it all. *It is finished!* No longer do we need to go through life wondering if we can live a life that can commend us to God. We can be confident of the eschatological verdict *now.* 'There is no condemnation for those who are in Christ Jesus.' (Romans 8:1) The *Einmaligkeit*, the 'once-for-allness' of salvation, achieved for us by the Lord himself, is what brings joy and assurance to the hearts of believers. A great many churchmen and women attend worship for decades without ever understanding that and revelling in its warmth. Preachers need to stress far more effectively, boldly and joyfully than they do, the 'finished work of Christ', God's decisive act for us to which we can make no contribution except our sins: we can only accept it or reject it.

But the same scriptures which are so clear about the once-for-allness of God's act for us are equally clear that we do not all perceive it in the twinkling of an eye. It may take years to percolate. And that is where the evangelist may go wrong. He or she may confuse the decisiveness and unrepeatableness of God's act with the way we respond. Sometimes the response is just as once-for-all and decisive and clear as God's act for us was. But sometimes it is like the sun gradually breaking through a cloudbank. Instant conversion is no part of evangelistic preaching. That can be manipulation. It can also be very discouraging to those who have come in a much more gradual way to perceive the glory of what God has done for them.

Continuous salvation

The evangelist must never forget that salvation is continuous. There are more references to the present tense of salvation than to its past aspect in the New Testament. That is why the more Catholic churchmanship prefers to speak of 'being in the way of salvation'. It is a helpful image. I am not where I was, an alien. I have gone through the door, which is Christ, and now I am travelling along the road called 'salvation' hand-in-hand with him and with fellow travellers. It is a long road, with many ups and downs, and I have not yet arrived at my goal. But I see it ahead of me and I press on towards it, constantly inviting others to join me on the journey. It might save us from a lot of disenchantment and a lot of falling away if there were less emphasis among evangelists on a one-off decision and a lot more on continuous discipleship which will not be complete until we see him face to face.

The future aspect

We would gain a wise perspective in evangelism if we were to regain the biblical balance on the past, present and future aspects of salvation. I remember learning many years ago this simple distinction between the tenses of salvation, and I have found, through subsequent study, that they are an accurate reflection of biblical teaching.

- *I have been saved* from the *penalty of sin* by Christ's death and resurrection.
- *I am being saved* from the *power of sin* (or not, as the case may be!) by the indwelling Holy Spirit.
- *I will be saved* from the *presence of sin* when I go to meet my Lord in the final resurrection.

Simple, but not simplistic. The future aspect of salvation is the goal towards which the whole creation moves, and we among it. If the idea of heaven and hell was overstressed in the Victorian age, it is unquestionably underplayed today, and if we are to be true to the biblical teaching on salvation it is very important to recover the Christian hope. No society can long survive without hope – and ours shows little sign of hope. This is an area where the gospel could be seen to be utterly relevant to our human dilemmas and despair. Nor can it be dismissed as pie in the sky, for it is authenticated by the historical events by which we date our era, and it is lived out in the Mother Teresas of this world.

Contextualising salvation

I find it fascinating that Jesus was able to come and proclaim God's salvation in a world where Jews and gentiles alike were all looking for salvation. The magicians and the politicians, the Zealots and the Pharisees, not to mention the man in the street fingering the coins which described the emperor as

106

'saviour of the world' – all these had different understandings of salvation, but Jesus was able to move in and be the fulfilment of those aspirations.

If we are to be effective in evangelism we need to be sensitive to the hungers of modern men and women, and discover where they provide an entry for the gospel. We see this process happening in the New Testament itself, as St John takes the synoptic language about the kingdom of God and transposes it, for the Graeco-Roman world for which he writes, into the politically non-inflammatory notion of eternal life, thus both retaining its essential meaning and clothing it in a phrase that made it immediately attractive to non-Christians. We need that same ability to translate not only words but ideas for our fellow citizens today, if we want them to find salvation.

'Non-spiritual' salvation

Salvation is not exclusively 'spiritual'. It was embarrassingly physical in the Old Testament, as we have seen: salvation from enemies, disease and death. It was, if possible, even more physical in the New Testament when the Saviour took human flesh. But we have drained that earthiness from it and turned it into something bloodless and 'spiritual'.

There were three very physical aspects to the salvation that the apostles preached. There was often healing, thus carrying on the healing aspect of Jesus' salvation. There was often exorcism, just as there was when Jesus proclaimed and enacted God's deliverance. And there was great care for human need, embodied so beautifully in the sharing of possessions and accommodation in the early Jerusalem Church, but by no means restricted to that. People are tired of words. We need to *show* the power of salvation, not just talk about it. And these three ways are still highly relevant. People need to find a community where they can experience healing, where dark spirits can be expelled from their lives, and where they can be liberated from materialism and can come to share, for sharing lies at the very heart of God. Exorcism, healing, and issues of peace, justice and caring are all important if the good news of salvation is to make a fresh impact on a jaded world.

Passing on salvation

Evangelism is imperative. The Church exists for two purposes: worship of God and witness to men. And the area of witness is often very weak, as it was with Israel of old. They were meant to embody and proclaim God's salvation among the pagan nations, yet this was one aspect (among several) of the role of 'Servant of the Lord' from which they shrank. We in the churches have been infected with Israel's disease – complacency. We have shrunk from passing on what God has given us. No wonder that, like manna kept for more than a day, it has gone bad on us. The Church will never be renewed until it goes out in evangelism as its Master did, as the apostles did, and as the growing churches, devoid of material possessions, but rich in spirit, do all over the two-thirds world. The link between salvation and evangelism is inseparable. And God will judge the Church – and the authors of this book – if we talk about it but do not do it. 'Just do it' – the bumper sticker has got it right!

> You are my witnesses, says the Lord, and my servant whom I have chosen, that you may know and believe me, and understand that I am He. Before me no god was formed, nor shall there be any after me. I, I am the Lord, and besides me there is no Saviour. I declared and saved and proclaimed, when there was no strange god among you *and you are my witnesses*, says the Lord. (Isaiah 49:10–12)

7 Salvation and Liberation*

Robinson Milwood

I am of the firm conviction that real theology and liberation must be fully contextualised. Salvation and liberation must be the experience and expression of a particular community and its people. Salvation and liberation ought to be the testimony, along with the confession of faith, of the people in their concrete situations. This must be their experience of the liberated Christ, sharing their daily lives through the power of his resurrection. The concept of salvation and liberation is applicable where communities are confronted with inimical challenges that are impediments to their development and growth. The fulfilment of both the individual and the community is to rejoice and to live and to serve in freedom, justice, equality and peace.

Paradoxically, it is in communities where people are denied certain basic human rights, such as proper housing, educational facilities and amenities, where the old always feel a sense of insecurity in the community, where racism is a daily reality, where children who have been retarded and amputated socially, emotionally, educationally, physically and spiritually are not able to grow in a caring environment, it is in these communities that society should be striving to provide salvation and liberation, not theoretically, but in a real human context.

Salvation and liberation are not illusions, whimsical dreams or imaginary things; rather they are the realities of human lives and conditions. Salvation and liberation should be lived out and expressed by the individual and the community, in worship, in caring, in serving and at times even

* © Robinson Milwood 1994

in suffering and dying for a cause. Such a definition of salvation and liberation is the hallmark of the London Mission Stoke Newington Circuit work. In this chapter my aim is to demonstrate and elucidate what I mean within the context of inner-city London, in the neighbourhood of Stoke Newington, which is in the deprived borough of Hackney.

Stoke Newington: the background

Stoke Newington is a multi-racial area in composition, with a large and visible population of West Indians, Asians and Africans. The indigenous white population that existed in Stoke Newington in the mid 1950s and late 1960s has become part of its history. The area is deeply economically depressed, in that poverty is evident and part of everyday life. Disillusionment, unemployment, frustration, racism, sexism, drug abuse, prostitution and violence are the current hallmarks of Stoke Newington. At the same time, the area is politically oppressed because of the local authority's political philosophy and policy. Even within a borough where there is tremendous poverty, it seems to many residents that they further create poverty to maintain their existence. The local authority, despite its limited budget, at times appears deliberately to deny better services and facilities in order to control enterprise, expansion and development. In many ways the authority gives the impression of being anti-success and anti-progress.

It is within this context that we are beginning to see the fruits of salvation and liberation. The Methodist Church in Stoke Newington is what I call the involved church, the sharing church, the pastoral church, the church that not only speaks of salvation and liberation but seeks to live out this concept for all of God's people. At times our approach may not be the traditional and conventional one, but the things we are seeking to do, and the movement we are involved in, are the ways in which we see the spirit of salvation and liberation reaching out to God's people, however hopeless their situation may appear, to give them hope and a new theology.

Worship

The Methodist Church in Stoke Newington is a traditional black Methodist church. We use the old hymn book because it is the one that we were all brought up on in the ministry, mission and witness of our church. We can identify in many ways with the spiritual vibrations and meanings of the hymns. When people sing 'Jesus keep me near the cross, There is a precious fountain', or 'Blessed assurance, Jesus is mine, Oh what a fore-taste of glory divine', or 'Peace, perfect peace, in this dark world of sin', or 'And if our fellowship here below in Jesus be so sweet, What heights of rapture shall we know when round his throne we meet', they are singing out of their own experience and context in Stoke Newington, because of the power of salvation and liberation that they feel. The Methodist faith and witness in this area is highly evangelical, not only because of its cultural affinity, but because the spirit of the risen Christ is in our worship as oppressed people. Salvation and liberation are causing people in our church to speak in tongues, to shout 'Hallelujah! Praise the Lord!', to clap hands, to shout praises to the living God. This is why there is no set time for our worship. It is so easy on a Sunday morning to worship for two-and-a-half or three hours non-stop, because the people are experiencing salvation and liberation. In the inner-city where oppression, alienation, selfishness, greed, hatred, bitterness, jealousy and racism are commonplace, the Methodist Church in Stoke Newington is known to be a preaching centre where the ordained and the lay alike are free – and feel free – to proclaim the gospel of the risen Christ, not intellectually or academically or through the virtue of various theological theories, but through their own personal encounter with the risen Christ, through sharing fellowship, human suffering and human pain.

Annual Pentecost celebration

Since 1979 we have been celebrating Pentecost in our Mission, in order to bring fellow Christians from different denominational, cultural, social and racial backgrounds to

111

meet as one people in the power of salvation and liberation, spiritually pregnant in our concept of Pentecost.

In our mission Pentecost is the time when people meet to recharge their batteries, spiritually, psychologically and intellectually in order to keep their physical engine in tip-top condition for the work of God. It is a time of equal participation in worship and mission work. It is a time of proclamation and re-affirmation of our faith and our experience and encounter with the risen Christ. In a local context where the church through its mission is seeking to bring hope to people in their everyday lives, it is a time of celebration as we endeavour to apply a new theological meaning and a new theological departure to the challenges of mission in the inner city. The problems are many, as we face the increasing use of drugs, prostitution, gambling, alcoholism, human violence, police brutality, harassment and misunderstanding. The old are growing disillusioned and dismayed as they face financial hardship because their dreams have been shattered by a government who has failed to make the poor their top priority on the agenda. Afro-West Indians, who have worked hard at jobs in the National Health Service and private industry to build a future out of nothing, are now becoming part of the forgotten people in the inner city, ignored, they feel, by both local and central government. Young people growing up here have a sense of hopelessness at the lack of job opportunities, decent homes and adequate local amenities and facilities. But in this situation of hopelessness, as God's people in Egypt often felt despair, the God of the Exodus spoke to us through out Pentecost celebration and our experience of salvation and liberation: 'I am come down to deliver them out of the land of oppression and alienation' (Exodus 3:8). 'The cry of my people in Stoke Newington is come unto me, and I have seen the oppression of my people.' This is how God is working through the risen Christ in our Mission.

Afro-Caribbean Thanksgiving service

The neighbourhood of Stoke Newington and our Mission is a significant witness that we are indeed a black, multi-racial church, with people from most of the Third World countries, and each year we hold a special cultural thanksgiving celebration when we remember our past history. We recall how God, through Christ, gave to our slave parents inner hope which became manifested in the great negro spiritual songs of old, songs which touched the heart of James Cone in his famous book *For My People*, and which inspired the mind of Martin Luther King when he gave that memorable speech in Washington, 'Free at last, free at last. Thank God Almighty we are free at last.'

Our Afro-Caribbean Thanksgiving Service is also the expression of our common lives, that we share the same history and the same humanity, and that we feel and know we have a mission to this pagan British society, this pagan city of London, that there is a mission for us to save our white brothers and sisters. We want to teach and show our white brothers and sisters the human capacity to love and to forgive, to teach them a new meaning, that we all emerged from the same potter's hand – Almighty God – and to demonstrate to them the meaning of reconciliation and to show that in Christ we are one. We can only speak with this tongue and with this language because we know and experience salvation and liberation.

The reality of salvation and liberation, therefore, is not something intellectual or academic. It is the inner experience of the heart and the soul. Rather than sermonising, we see our Afro-Caribbean Thanksgiving Service as a time of rejoicing, a time of thanksgiving and a time of celebration.

Pastoral Counselling Unit

It is an often heard claim by politicians and institutions, particularly financial institutions, that we in Britain are an opulent society. Whilst wealth may be visible in certain parts of our country, there can be no political or theological denial of the evidence of human suffering – oppression, alienation, selfishness, hatred, jealousy, bitterness and racism – all around us. In the midst of this, the indigent have no voice and even the Church that ought to be the voice of the poor is becoming voiceless or, at best, muted in its protest.

I see around me in Stoke Newington today young people who are mentally and emotionally unstable, and adults in their mid-forties and early fifties equally psychologically and emotionally disturbed. This is why the Mission Pastoral Counselling Unit is so vitally important. Through the Unit many have received, and are continuing to receive, the experience of inner salvation and liberation.

Over twelve months ago, a young man in his early twenties came to see me in my Counselling Surgery. He lived in Enfield and he had travelled to Stoke Newington because he had heard about our Unit. I said, 'Brother, what can I do for you?' He sat down and he paused for approximately three minutes. Then he looked at me and said, 'Reverend, I have come to you for help.' I asked him what help he needed from me. He said, 'Look at me. That is my need.' He showed me his police record. His life had been dominated by crime. He was looking like a prodigal son – rejected, disillusioned, frightened and hopeless. I read his report with pain in my heart and tears in my eyes, because as I read, it reminded me of so many other cases, of the many schools and institutions in Britain that have destroyed the future and lives of so many young people out of racial ignorance.

I said to the young man, 'If you are prepared to work with me, and to start to build a new life, I will help you.' Without any hesitation he agreed and said that all he wanted was one more chance with his life. In reading his police records, I discovered that he was a trained youth leader and I asked him if he loved children. He said he did and that he had a six-month-old child of his own. I told him that I would give him a chance in one of our day nurseries, under my own personal supervision and counselling.

In February 1994, at a staff meeting, the young man confessed that he had found a new life and that he had discovered himself anew. He had found inner peace and freedom in his soul. He is now rapidly developing as a very committed and efficient day nursery carer.

I tell this story for one simple reason: to show that salvation and liberation are not to be found in academic or theological text-books, but in people's lives, encounters and relationships, and in the act of worship in prayer and devotion of a Christian's life in the Church.

Educational Institute

Five years ago the Mission set up a special Educational Institute as part of its programme to provide education and tuition for adults, particularly in the field of Religious Studies. The Institute is linked to Birkbeck College, University of London. Students have the freedom to pursue a certificate or a diploma course by studying any four from a range of subjects on offer. These include biblical studies, church history and issues such as the philosophy and sociology of religion.

This is just the foundation stone for students to build on as they wish, perhaps by taking a BA or a BD degree course and possibly moving on to a Master's degree in any given subject. What is of tremendous importance is that the lay members of the Mission have the opportunity to gain theological knowledge which is so vitally important to the individual's faith. From September 1994, the Mission Educational institute is embarking on a new phase of educational and theological empowerment of the poor.

Educational and theological empowerment of the poor

This new departure will be led by two past students of the Institute who have obtained Master's degrees in Theology, and who will teach introductory courses in Religious Studies at the Institute. The opportunity is there for young graduates to lecture for three to five years in the Institute, and after that period, to be recommended by the Principal of the Institute to Birkbeck College to be considered as a recognised lecturer. These people will then be able to go to other centres in London to continue teaching or to develop new centres in the city, thereby expanding the mission and ministry of educational and theological empowerment of the poor to the laity who come into contact with this approach to mission. People will then begin to see and feel the vibrations of salvation and liberation in their lives and around them.

The Methodist Church in Stoke Newington has a defini-
tive programme of educational and theological empowerment of the poor for the circuit and beyond. Politically, in
Stoke Newington education is looked upon by the local
authority with very little appreciation and importance.
People tell me that to find a decent school in Stoke Newington is very difficult, and that to find a school with discipline
and social and religious rectitude is a foreign thing here in
many ways. Politically, in the opinion of many I meet, the
word 'excellence' holds no meaning for the local authority.
Parents have grown disillusioned and powerless. Young
people have grown up in Hackney without any proper educational foundation. Over ninety-five per cent of black boys
in Stoke Newington have a police record somewhere along
the line in their lives. The majority of young blacks in Stoke
Newington share the common experience of receiving very
limited educational support and encouragement from their
schools. Young boys and girls have grown up to know only
one thing – unemployment and early motherhood or father-
hood, without any moral responsibility because of the conditions that have denied them any aspirations, any goals in
life, and have provided very few role models for them. It
is in this atmosphere that Stoke Newington Mission has
developed its agenda and – thanks be to God for the divine
mandate through God's people – is working towards educational and theological empowerment of the poor.

Stoke Newington Mission Montessori Day Nurseries

The Circuit Meeting of the Mission accepted the gigantic
challenge eight years ago that we as a Mission must give
priority to education for children. To this end, we had been
profoundly supported financially and otherwise by the
London Committee of the Methodist Church, which helped
us to create adequate facilities to serve the church and the
community. We now have two day nurseries in our Mission,
with a staff of more than thirty-five full-time workers, providing day care for children and allowing their parents to return
to college or to gain job experience or employment. The
children are provided with professional child-care in an

environment that is prepared specifically to assist in their intellectual, physical, emotional, psychological and spiritual development. The standard of child-care, which is church-based, is salvation and liberation for the parents. They can see what I call 'the church love in action, the church faith in action, the gospel in action, the spirit bearing witness in action'.

The Mission is providing a service because the local authority in many ways has failed to provide suitable facilities in child-care. We saw a human need, and the church has responded to that need, where parents had seen and experienced only darkness and hopelessness, a bleak future for their children. Parents are now appreciative that the Methodist Church exists in the community. It is the church of action, the church with a mission, with a set agenda; it is a church with Exodus people.

Empowerment of the laity

In many ways the Church has been tied to structures that alienate people, structures that have become institutionalised and that relate ineffectively to people, structures that are pedantic and far removed in relevance from people's everyday experiences. This is why empowerment of the laity is so essential to the Mission strategy in Stoke Newington. Here the laity is not only given the freedom to become stewards and local officers and secretaries in the church, but also the freedom to own their church and to claim their heritage in the church. With the freedom that salvation and liberation bring, people are learning a new experience. They are learning the responsibility of stewardship and of what it is to be a servant of the Church and a servant of Christ. They are learning that empowerment of the poor means many things – hard work, blood, sweat and tears, perseverance, and putting their hands into situations that are, by sociological definition, untouchable.

The laity is learning also to share in the power of the Church. One example of this is the training of new members. This is no longer the responsibility of the minister; it is the responsibility of Sister A. A. Fashade, MA, one of our recognised and distinguished local preachers, who is also a nursing officer. She is a graduate of our Educational Institute. It is her job to train all newcomers into membership of the Church. Another example is our Saturday School, where boys and girls are able to come for extra lessons and tuition. This is being provided by one of our lay preachers, Mr Jonathon Miller, BEd, along with Mrs Jean Pottinger, a white indigenous mother who came into contact with our mission work a few years ago and immediately recognised that she had a contribution to make and that the mission atmosphere was what she was looking for. With this type of team work, there is added salvation and liberation for the underprivileged.

The Women's Fellowship

The Women's Fellowship is a very important arm of our mission work. It is well organised and highly professional in its work, whether this is conducting church and mission functions and various services, or helping the elderly, providing meals at festive seasons for the poor, and visiting the housebound and the lonely. No wonder it was women who first received the good news and communicated the message 'He is risen' to the world. Just as women began to share in the ministry of Jesus, so their place is recognised in the function of this Mission. This is salvation and liberation at work in team-work, partnership and sharing.

Ecumenical witness

Some fourteen years ago, when the Mission began to accommodate and to work with black church leaders, it was an unusual occurrence, but now it is commonplace to see various black-led churches not only using the Mission church premises, but sharing in services and events to expand the kingdom of God. So this is proudly a black ecumenical communion with a mission to a dying and perishing neighbourhood and a dying and perishing inner city. This black ecumenical movement is divinely appointed. The challenges are there, but we accept them because we are sent by the risen Christ to offer his salvation and liberation to people in the inner city whose lives had been overtaken by materialism, secularism, self-centredness and human greed.

The poor and reconciliation

Although the poor – marginalised and oppressed – are experiencing great hardship, deprivation and political and economic stagnation and powerlessness, at the same time we, the poor, believe in the praxis of reconciliation. We acknowledge that we live in a divided society, but the Christ we know is a reconciling Christ, a Christ who is there through us to break down all barriers, to shake hands and to embrace even the enemy, to demonstrate love in a positive way, and always to offer forgiveness and peace. There is a strange paradox. The poor have inner power and strength because the salvation and liberation that they know through Christ is always sustaining. The poor live with a deep eschatological hope, despite the oppression, persecution and rejection. 'And God shall wipe away all tears from their eyes. There shall be no more death, neither sorrow, nor crying, neither shall there be any more pain for the former things are passed away' (Revelation 21:4).

It is words like these that give to the hearts of the poor a deep sense of hope. Although the structures of British society are designed to alienate, segregate and isolate people and to turn people into selfish individuals, the poor find a renewed strength to bring harmony where disharmony has existed for a long time. They find strength to bring concord where racism has divided people, and where, in our society today, for many economic stagnation is a fact of life and is causing untold suffering to the poor, the fatherless, the homeless, the unemployed, the single parents. 'Who shall separate us from the love of Christ?' The poor will continue to encounter 'tribulations, distress, persecution, famine, nakedness, peril and even the sword' of human hatred (Romans 8:35). But the poor have within their hearts the knowledge and awareness that nothing is able to separate us from the love of God, which together we can find in Christ Jesus our Lord.

The power of the gospel

Jesus came into Galilee announcing salvation and liberation (Mark 1:14–15). Stoke Newington Mission is continuing to announce the good news that God's kingdom is realised here and now in the ministry of the Mission. The gospel is both a proclaimed gospel and a lived gospel. It is the salvation and liberation that Jesus brings to his oppressed people through the ministry and mission of his Church. The gospel is the content of the true meaning of resurrection. The gospel in our context is the expression of love that speaks from the cross. It is love in action. It is love unconditionally. It is love with responsibility. It is love with priorities and with a consummation goal in mind, that surrenders all into the hands of Almighty God. The gospel is lived by the people in their Christian witness, in their treatment of each other, their respect for their community, their commitment to the Church, and the personal sacrifice and pain that comes with the proclamation and the living out of the gospel of Jesus. It is a gospel of bearing the cross with him who came to and for the poor. Because of this experience, the Mission and its people are able to confess, without any reservation, their real experience of Isaiah 61:1–3:

> The spirit of the Lord God is upon me; because the Lord hath anointed me to preach good tidings unto the meek; he hath sent me to bind up the brokenhearted, to proclaim liberty to the captives, and the opening of the prison to them that are bound;
>
> To proclaim the acceptable year of the Lord, and the day of vengeance of our God; to comfort all that mourn;
>
> To appoint unto them that mourn in Zion, to give unto them beauty for ashes, the oil of joy for mourning, the garment of praise for the spirit of heaviness; that they might be called trees of righteousness, the planting of the Lord, that he might be glorified.

In this chapter, I have deliberately and consciously avoided any deep theological reflections and concentration, or any philosophical speculation. I have tried to express what salvation means for us, to live with salvation and liberation beside us. For the Mission of Stoke Newington salvation and liberation have come to mean that Christ is alive and that the Church has a mission and a ministry to perform. Salvation and liberation mean for us that as a mission circuit we must endeavour to stir the conscience of this community, to challenge the local structures that perpetually amputate human goals and development. Salvation and liberation mean for us that we must not bend the back, we must stand tall in our faith. Salvation and liberation mean for us that we should never retreat, never surrender the principles of the gospel of Christ, never surrender the place of the Church. Indeed, we stand to defend the Church, we stand as a body of Methodist people who are able to say, through our salvation and liberation experience, 'our eyes have seen the glory of the coming of the Lord'.

> Peace, perfect peace,
> Our future all unknown?
> Jesus we know,
> And he is on the throne.
>
> It is enough:
> Earth's struggles soon shall cease,
> And Jesus calls us
> To heaven's perfect peace.

So, with salvation and liberation as our tools, along with the gospel of Jesus, we shall continue to dream great dreams. We shall continue in our visions, we shall continue with conviction and through our experience, the work we have begun for Christ and the Methodist Church.

> When we walk with the Lord,
> In the light of his word,
> What a glory he sheds on our way.
> While we do his good will
> He abides with us still
> And all who will trust and obey.

Part 3

The Modern Challenge

8 Salvation and Political Justice*

Sehon Goodridge

It is generally agreed that theories of salvation have been in large measure individualistic, and have conditioned much thinking of salvation as concerned solely with each individual's behaviour, the pilgrimage of each autonomous soul, responding to God's gracious action in Jesus Christ. Important as the individual's response is, salvation cannot be attained without communion with, and service to, our fellow human beings. It is this understanding of the corporate nature of God's salvific act in Christ, who has assumed our total humanity and inaugurated a new creation, that enables us to see the limitations of purely individualistic views of salvation, concerned in particular contexts with the rescue from mortality and ignorance, guilt and punishment, despair and meaninglessness. We can perceive and experience salvation as total liberation of total persons in their total contexts. Since no man or woman is an island, none of us can be saved on our own; we can only be made whole in solidarity with others, and with the transformation of socio-economic and political structures and institutions, in order that life may flourish for all. For this reason John Macquarrie has asserted that the idea of individual salvation is a contradiction in terms.[1]

With this political vision and dimension we seek to provide a needful balance to narrowly conceived individualistic notions of salvation. Human beings are essentially social, and as political animals we need the *polis*, government and all the machinery and mechanisms of a structured society, for a purposeful and fulfilled life. John de Gruchy, writing

* © Sehon Goodridge 1994

125

in the context of South Africa, calls our attention to this inescapable aspect of human life:

> The *polis* is the city, that is, the arena of human social transactions affecting the common life of the community in all its dimensions. A moment's reflection will show that nothing is excluded from the *polis*, and therefore nothing is exempt from politics – the art of keeping society functioning properly. Everything from family life to education, from daily bread to economic policies is included. Cabinet portfolios touch on every aspect of existence, and some aspects are at their mercy. The church itself does not escape, nor can it, for it too falls within the *polis*. And insofar as the church is a vitally interested partner in the life of people, there must inevitably be some kind of relationship between Church and State. This means that the church is involved in politics, whether it wants to be or not. The important consideration is the nature of that relationship.[2]

De Gruchy has clearly stated the political imperative from which we cannot flinch. Writing in the Caribbean context, I have also affirmed this imperative:

> Any concern for the right ordering of the world, of society and the events of men inevitably commits the church to a political task – political not in the sense of party-politics, but in the sense of participating in the struggle of the powerless and penniless for liberation. For the church to seek an area of operation free of political commitment is a false paradise which does not exist. The alternatives are now clear: either we support the continuation of oppression or we struggle for liberation. We will support one or the other by the way we preach, teach, worship, use our money, speak or remain silent.[3]

It is good to have the opportunity to address this subject in a different context. But before I do so, it is necessary to examine some dichotomies that may get in the way.

First, is the task of evangelism to change people themselves or to change society? It is sometimes argued that Christ changes the individual's heart, mind and spirit; changed individuals will inevitably lead to a changed society. When we consider, however, a world of relationships very often characterised by dominance and dependence, power and powerlessness, superiority and inferiority, it is vital that conversion is fleshed out to incorporate this dimension. The emergence of a new vision of humanity sustained by justice, peace and love, and the dawn of a new social order and a new world order marked by a feeling of co-humanity and interdependence, that we are our brothers' and sisters' keepers, that we are in one world, created and restored by God's saving activity: is this not total salvation? Does this not put the burden of proof on those who uphold a political structure that maintains oppression, exploitation or racial discrimination? Is this not evidence of sin in the very structure of society, from which men and women yearn and struggle to be freed? Political structures and institutions are created to serve human life, but if they deviate from this proper end and acquire a life of their own, they enslave and dehumanise human beings. Life becomes a conflict, injustice is institutionalised, and salvation becomes synonymous with liberation. Gustavo Gutiérrez, one of the founding fathers of Liberation Theology, clinches this point as he describes why he uses the word 'liberation': (1) it points to the conflictive nature of the present reality, i.e. the conflict of the poor classes with regard to the wealthy and powerful; (2) it implies a new consciousness, which leads human beings to be subjects of their own history, and thus 'leads to the creation of a new man and a qualitatively different society'; and (3) it demonstrates a deeper relation to the biblical sources and to the liberating life and death of Christ.[4]

Secondly, is sin individual or collective? Properly speaking, sin is a personal action of disobedience and rebellion against the known will of our loving and gracious God. An offence against our neighbours is also an offence against God. Apathy, indifference and irresponsibility are all forms of sin. So too is our failure to act justly and to serve the least of our brothers and sisters in the human family. We begin to see that what we do, or fail to do, can affect others, for we are persons-in-community. What is worse, we can collude with, and participate in, the injustice of a situation from which we benefit and derive power and privilege. For instance, if some people in a dominant group feel secure in an ideology of power, control and racial superiority, they

127

will collude with racism and may themselves practise racial discrimination. Our personal sins can indeed affect attitudes and practices in society. We can be conditioned by a group ideology that influences our dispositions and actions. Individuals are responsible for what they do, or fail to do, but their actions or inactions can assume corporate dimensions and even lead to institutional injustice in various forms of disability, discrimination and dehumanisation. From all these, good Lord, deliver us, individually and collectively!

Thirdly, is salvation temporal or eternal? There is the view that God's work of salvation concerns our eternal destiny. We come from God and we go to God. Our 'souls' are on their spiritual and eternal destiny. While there is a profound truth here, it is not the whole truth. We are not dualities of souls and bodies; we are total persons. Our bodies are integral to our personalities. We are able to exist and relate in time and space. As psychosomatic beings we have an intricate mind-spirit-body relationship, each affecting the others. Our wholeness, our health, depends upon this proper and positive relationship. A healthy relationship with our environment and material context is also important. Festering poverty, deprivation and disease count against the flourishing of human life. We are horrified by scenes of children and adults in many parts of the world emaciated by physical disadvantage and disease, and we join their cry for deliverance. We may even feel the anger and outrage, and have to face squarely the question: How can we justify God to such persons? The cries go up: Why? How long? Such yearnings for a quality of life must certainly fall within the salvific activity of God. Eternal life is God's offer of a quality of life with him, which is both spiritual and temporal. It is not either/or, but both/and! Pierre Bigo helps us to focus this balance:

> All that many Christians relate to their salvation is their inner and family life and some attitudes about giving individual help to others. As elements within the compass of salvation, only love, sin, and prayer count with them. They therefore exclude, if not their professional life, at least anything that has to do with politics. When we are aware of the importance of 'the political' in

the creation of any new human relation, we recognize that such a view is an aberration. In the political area, perhaps more than in any other, a person's eternal destiny is decided. We have to conclude that the work of salvation, because it does concern eternity, has much to do with temporal affairs, which are oriented to building up an earthly city. The Christian message, because it holds out an eternal hope to the poor, gives them a human hope right now: it invites people to establish a relationship and build a city where the poor will not be exploited and will feel at home.[5]

Fourthly, there is the question of God or Caesar. We have to resolve this complex: 'Render to Caesar the things that are Caesar's and to God the things that are God's' (Mark 12:17; Matthew 22:21; Luke 20:25). This was Jesus' reply to a catch-question posed by a group who had opposite views on one of the most burning issues of the day. In Judaea, under Roman occupation, ought a patriotic Jew to pay the poll-tax? Was our Lord for the Zealot resistance movement? Or was he guarding the status quo? Whichever way he answered he would be caught. The answer he gave has become proverbial. What did Jesus mean? Some have quoted this text as the authority for keeping religion out of politics, as though there were two separate compartments – 'public affairs that belong to Caesar' and 'spiritual matters that belong to God'. Politics is a dirty game; keep out of it! But can we keep out of politics? We have to eat, work, provide for our families, and have the amenities and services that make life worth living. It is the responsibility of any government to provide for the essential needs of all its citizens. But the State, like the Church, must not outreach its servant-nature. The coin with the image of Caesar's head on it is legal tender; pay him his due. But do not for the sake of political advantage withhold from God what belongs to him. What belongs to God? Everything, including Caesar. The issue is not the recognition of 'the separation of powers' or the demarcation of 'two orders'. Nor is the issue that of a frontier dispute between two rival authorities. The issue is that no human authority, civil or ecclesiastical, is ultimate. Both are under the sovereignty of God. In the arena of God's creative and re-creative activity there is no distinction between the sacred and the secular. The God and Caesar tension is resolved in a life of utter loyalty to God. The Church must require Christians to obey the State, so long as the State itself recognises its own limitations, and allows the Church political freedom to proclaim and practise its gospel of liberation.

We have examined some dichotomies and have concluded that they are not helpful in our consideration of the social and public – the political – aspect of salvation. Paul Avis shares our conviction that such dichotomies must be discarded:

> What is required, as I see it, is a holistic interpretation of the atonement in which the dichotomies that have been exploited between objective and subjective atonement and between the person and the work of Christ are healed. It is the total performance of the life and destiny of Jesus, received as the Christ within the church which is his resurrection body, and made effectual through the Holy Spirit, that constitutes the atonement. . . .[6]

We are in a position to affirm unreservedly that the realm of the public, the political, does not fall outside God's saving activity. A cursory glance at the biblical record reminds us that God has always been present in political events, in deliverance, upheaval, invasion, defeat, reconstitution and restoration. When the Bible speaks of God it is not afraid to do so in political language. It talks about covenant – a 'treaty' – that God initiates and gives to his people to enable them to make a response to him and live in relationships of mutuality and reciprocity. The Bible also speaks of a God who has given human beings responsibility for the right ordering of society. But, alas, they have not accepted this responsibility. They have passed the buck, become slothful and apathetic. This is indeed the political sin! Harvey Cox is right to call our attention to it: 'Man's existence is by its very nature life with and for the fellowman. This makes it essentially political. The apathetic avoidance of politics is the sophisticated way in which we, like Cain, club our brothers to death.'[7]

Whether we are active or inactive in the political sphere,

our lives have political influence. The Bible never separates the personal from the social. We are confronted by the prophetic memory and imagination: 'He has showed you, O man, what is good; and what does the Lord require of you but to do justice and to love kindness, and to walk humbly with your God?' (Micah 6:8; cf. Amos 5:21–24; Isaiah 1:15). We remember also the good news which ushered in God's kingly rule: 'The spirit of the Lord is upon me, because he has anointed me to preach good news to the poor. He has sent me to proclaim release to the captives and recovering of sight to the blind, to set at liberty those who are oppressed, to proclaim the acceptable year of the Lord.' (Luke 4:18–19)

At this point an excursion into Liberation Theology will prove most illuminating, for we shall discover that it is not enough to interpret the world, but that we must change it. We meet a God who defends and liberates the poor and oppressed, exacting justice and inaugurating the kingdom. As José Miranda affirms:

> When God intervenes, his principal activity is directed to the conscience. And through people's consciences he achieves his true intervention . . . The God of the Exodus is the God of conscience. The Liberation of the slaves from Egypt was principally a work of the imperative of liberty and justice inculcated into the Israelites.[8]

Here is a cogent expression of liberation ethics which challenges us to rediscover the place of justice within our Christian tradition. We tend to be wary of the use of the word 'justice' less we be branded as Socialists or Marxists. But we must remember that justice is part of our tradition. Indeed justice and love bear a dialectical relationship; we cannot have one without the other. They are like Darby and Joan! There is a Christian socialism that is admirably like that of the revered Brazilian ecclesiastic and theologian Dom Helder Camara, who writes: 'My socialism is a special one which respects the human person and turns to the gospel. My socialism is justice.'[9]

Miranda also sees the gospel as salvation, because it reveals

131

God's justice which delivers us from his wrath against injustice, inter-human injustice.[10] He argues that God's justice has come through the death and resurrection of Christ, which gives faith 'its capacity to make men just'. It was necessary that the Law crucify Christ that we may be free from the Law:

> When before your eyes the law crucifies . . . the only man who did not know sin, God destroys sins and the law for ever. At this point the justice of God begins in history and the 'justice' of law ends.[11]

We have seen a demonstration of the inner interaction between theology and ethics. We are summoned to have a mature understanding of Christianity and its relationship to the world. It is not a narrowly idealist and privatised morality, but a morality that is social and public, and thus political.

With the enormity and complexity of contemporary issues and challenges, Christians cannot claim to be wiser than the experts in politics, sociology and economics. For this reason some of our contemporaries would argue that the gospel is to change people, and that political involvement is divisive. True, there can be bad meddling in politics when we do not take the trouble to get the facts based on hard research and analysis, when we jump on the bandwagon, when we get involved in power struggle for personal aggrandisement, or when we fail to listen to the gospel in our rush to do justice. To avoid this bad form of 'playing politics', we must acquire the perception of political responsibility in a carefully critical and self-critical manner. In this regard I have written elsewhere:

> It is true that traditional conceptions show no clear grasp of the weight of the political implications of Christianity and yet it is incumbent upon the Church to ask concerning every field, including politics, what is the purpose of God for it. Now for the Church to ask this sort of question, does not mean that it must take sides, for its members are spread throughout the political spectrum, so that there is no question of party-politics . . . it must be maintained that the understanding which the Church has

concerning the nature and destiny of man gives it a qualification for deciding what kind of structure is wholesome for men and what is unwholesome. When the Church addresses itself to the right ordering of society for man in his sin, then the Church is exercising its political responsibility.[12]

The relationship between Church and State is not simply one of mutual self-interest: the religious realm protected and the political order legitimated. A significant critique has been made by theologians in Southern Africa of the nature of this relationship. In the *Kairos Document* there is a cutting assessment of both 'State Theology' and 'Church Theology'. 'State Theology' is seen as the theological justification of the *status quo* with its racism, capitalism and totalitarianism, blessing injustice and canonising the interest and will of the powerful, and reducing the poor to subservience and non-personhood.

> How does 'State Theology' do this? It does this by misusing theological concepts and biblical texts for its own political purposes. In this document we would like to draw your attention to four key examples of how this is done in South Africa. The first would be the use of Romans 13:1–7 to give absolute and 'divine' authority to the State. The second would be the use of the idea of 'Law and Order' to determine and control what the people may be permitted to regard as just and unjust. The third would be the use of the word 'Communism' to brand anyone who rejects 'State Theology'. And finally there is the use that is made of the name of God.[13]

In a critique of 'Church Theology' the Document poses the pertinent challenge:

> Why then does 'Church Theology' appeal to the top rather than to the people who are suffering? Why does this theology not demand that the oppressed stand up for their rights and wage a struggle against their oppressors? Why does it not tell them that it is *their* duty to work for justice and to change the unjust structures? Perhaps the answer to these questions is that appeals from the 'top' in the church tend very easily to be appeals to the 'top' in society. An appeal to the conscience of those who perpetuate the system of injustice must be made. But real change

and true justice can only come from below, from the people –
most of whom are Christians.[14]

Over against a theology that legitimates the structures of
power and racial superiority, there is the theology of the
'people of the land', the poor and the oppressed. This
preferential option for the poor commits us to take seriously
the experiences of poor people and to allow this experience
to shape our reflection and action. Such people's theology
is not done *for* the poor, but *with* and *from* the poor. The
poor become our evangelisers and our values of power and
privilege are subverted. We can imagine how subversive Jesus
must have seemed to the religious establishment of his day.
The 'crowd' are the privileged ones; they are endowed with
God's gifts to be true subjects of their history. They may
include 'publicans and sinners' but they are summoned to
destiny in Jesus Christ in whose presence, ministry and
saving activity they witness the unmasking and dethroning
of those rebellious powers which enslave, divide and
dehumanise. They experience liberation and vindication.
The crushed and put down can stand tall and raise their
heads, for God certainly lifts up the lowly.

This has been a definite theme in the black religious
experience; from slavery to emancipation, liberation and
celebration. In the experience of the demonic institution of
human slavery, black people kept hope alive in the 'invisible
institution', in the 'arbour church' singing and drumming
and dancing, well into the night. People who were held as
property, with no human rights, and denied the opportunity
to read and write, yet heard the biblical stories from the
galleries of the master's church, wove them into their experience of suffering and struggle and projected the great hope
of God's liberation. The negro spirituals must be set in this
context and be appreciated as liberation songs, and not be
spiritualised and privatised. They were songs that challenged
the ideology and morphology of the master class. Take, for
instance, the following spiritual:

Go down Moses, way down in Egypt's land,
Tell old Pharoah, To let my people go.
When Israel was in Eygpt's land, Let my people go!

Oppressed so hard they could not stand, Let my people go!
Thus saith the Lord, bold Moses said, Let my people go!
If not I'll smite your first-born dead, Let my people go!
No more bondage shall they toil, Let my people go!
Let them come out with Egypt's spoil, Let my people go!

This spiritual is obviously about God as the liberator of the Israelites from Egypt – the Exodus. But it is also a song of encouragement and confidence of what God will still do for the oppressed. The story of the text and the story of a people's experience of oppression are interwoven and the hope of liberation is kept alive. Experience, biblical story, faith: were these black slaves the first Liberation Theologians?

Black religious experience and worship have often been criticised as being too spiritual, emotional and other-worldly. But such criticism is a failure to understand the admixture of survival and liberation, conformity and political protest, in much of black religion. Gayraud Wilmore sets this criticism to rest:

> What may be called the liberation tradition in black religion also begins with the determination to survive, but because it is exterior rather than primarily interior (and for that reason its carriers find more space in which to manoeuvre) it goes beyond strategies of sheer survival to strategies of elevation – from 'make do' to 'must do more'. Both strategies are basic to Afro-American life and culture. They are intertwined in complex ways throughout the history of the diaspora. Both are responses to reality in a dominating white world. . . .[15]

Wilmore gives us a well-documented historical overview of the involvement of black religious groups and individuals in efforts to bring about political and social change in America. The black movement for racial justice in the 1960s was in large measure nurtured and inspired by the black Christian experience in the Black Church in the South. Martin Luther King Jr and his companions in the struggle were living testimony to this fact. The civil rights movement was anchored in the Black Church, organised by black ministers and laity, and supported financially by black church members.

King clearly understood justice as an integral part of salvation, as he was confronted by *the* paradox: black people had sought their goals through love and moral persuasion, devoid of power; white people had sought their goals through power, devoid of love. As he saw it, herein lay the conflict of immoral power with powerless morality. For him, power was the ability to bring about social, political and economic changes. For him, justice and love were inseparable: power is love implementing justice, and justice is love correcting everything that stands against love. Power without love is reckless and abusive, and love without power is sentimental and anaemic. King could not, therefore, flinch from his responsibility to summon black people to assess their political and economic strength in order to achieve their legitimate goal of justice 'in the land of the free and the home of the brave'. May his dream live on!

> I have a dream that one day my children will no longer be judged by the color of their skin but by the content of their character.[16]

King was certain that 'We shall overcome'.

Salvation includes liberation from all those forces that frustrate and dominate. When such forces incarnate and manifest themselves in the structures of society, then the kingdoms of this world need to be restored to their servant-nature, and become the kingdom of our Lord and his Christ. Jesus' enactment of this 'unworldly' kingdom is of political significance in the world. Its enactment is a challenge and a rebuke to all worldly power systems. He therefore makes the firm political assertion, 'My kingdom is not of this world' (John 18:36). Those who follow him and face the demands of the kingdom must learn to distance themselves from the false security of wealth, the insatiable quest for power and the debilitating preoccupation with worldly care. The politics of the kingdom is a distinctive type of politics, the politics of the cross, the power of suffering and service on behalf of human liberation and reconciliation. We turn to Jürgen Moltmann for an excellent explication of the political consequences of the cross:

> For believers, Christ crucified was made the righteousness of

God, and for them political authority was deprived of its religious sanction. Christ, crucified in powerlessness and shame, has become their highest authority. Consequently, they no longer believe in religio-political authority, for the anxiety and fear that demanded it has been eliminated. Modern political theology considers the mortal conflict of Jesus with the public powers of his day to be central. Such conflict played no part in the old political theology that developed 'State metaphysics'. The only question is how this conflict of Jesus with the public powers can today be expressed in individual Christian and ecclesial public life.[17]

Here is no advocation of violence, nor is there a call to the Church to rule the world. Rather it is a reminder that political institutions, and the Church itself, stand in the light of the cross and under the judgement of the kingdom of justice, peace and love. The conflict that is waged is against 'principalities and powers' which can frustrate, but will not count ultimately against the justice of God. Paul reminds us that on the cross Christ 'disarmed the principalities and powers and made a public example of them, triumphing over them in him' (Colossians 2:15). Of course the crucifixion and resurrection of Christ must be held together in this one salvific act. The cross of Jesus Christ is both the context of, and the way to, his resurrection. To live under the cross is the characteristic of the struggle in which action is not doomed to failure; to live by the resurrection is also a characteristic of the struggle in which hope springs eternal. Political theologies have maintained an emphasis that God is involved in the changes of the world, not trying only to reflect these changes, but to show the immanence of the cross and resurrection of Jesus Christ. For this reason André Dumas concludes:

> Finally, there must certainly be a connection between theology and politics. A theology which is not political is limited to the mysteries of the soul. Human personality gains nothing from such schizophrenia between religion as a private affair and politics as a secular, secularized, atheistic affair . . . I also believe that any theology which is not political lacks the assurance given by the

events of the cross and resurrection, that it is in contact with reality.[18]

God is at work in the whole of history, including the realm of politics, and hope is born of the cross. The total Christ-event causes the Church, in the power of the Spirit, to bear witness to the kingdom in the here and now, and this witness prepares the way for the kingdom to come. The ultimate wholeness and completeness – *shalom* – is beyond us, but we can have a foretaste of it in our time.

If a foretaste of this *shalom* is denied human beings because of oppression, exploitation or discrimination, how is change to be realised? If there is injustice in the system, constituting 'primary violence', are human beings justified in resorting to 'secondary violence' as a last resort when all avenues for communication and redress are closed? We do not have sufficient space here to deal adequately with these questions, but some discussion, however brief, is necessary. There are many just causes in our world as injustice takes one form or another. In some places only struggle and pressure seem to be the means of change. But is violence the only answer? Only in limited contexts, after all legal and constitutional means have been tried, can there be any excuse for violence, as a last resort. Even then the principles of proportionality and immunity must not be discarded. There is no doubt that violence can be done to the person because of unemployment, deprivation, oppression, police brutality, torture and unfair imprisonment. The denial of basic civil and political rights can indeed constitute primary violence, evoking secondary violence, and in turn counter-violence, and the escalation of violence continues in a vicious circle until we have a spiral of violence.

Is there another option? There is the option of non-violence. Despite attempts to paint a picture of 'Jesus the Zealot', the violent revolutionary, the total picture of Jesus shows one who did not opt for the short-cut of violence, but the long and patient road of transforming love and suffering. Though he resisted the temptation to exercise his responsibility of bringing in the kingdom by violent methods, he did not opt for social withdrawal or ecclesiastical conservatism.[19] When he said 'Do not resist one who is evil' (Matthew 5:39), he was not advocating a policy of non-resistance, but a policy of not resisting evil by evil means. In this Jesus tradition non-violent action on the social, economic and political level has taken the form of peaceful protest, demonstration, boycott and non-co-operation. Mohandas Gandhi and Martin Luther King Jr are two sterling examples of leaders who have chosen the option of non-violence. Non-violent resistance requires much discipline. Gandhi's ashrams, his dedication to the truth and his inspiration drawn from the Sermon on the Mount, provided him with this. King's Christian commitment to justice and love undergirded his practice of non-violent resistance. While refusing to use the weapons of violence Christians have a responsibility to be the conscience of society by displaying a social structure through which the gospel works to change demonic structures of power. Christians are called to demonstrate the responsible society, the kind of society in which there are no social, economic and racial inequalities.

What an opportunity we have to participate in God's act of saving the world which he still loves so much! The salvation that he brings is not to be privatised. It is public and all-embracing. We are restored to personal integrity in body, mind and spirit, and are related to each other, and to all others, without confusion or separation. We come to know that we are essentially persons-in-community, and that we shall be saved in solidarity with each other. In God's creative and liberative activity, there is no place for dichotomies between the individual and the corporate, the spiritual and the material, the temporal and the eternal, the sacred and the profane. There is no area of life, no part of history, no section of creation, that falls outside his saving grace. Sin in all its aspects affects not only individuals, but also structures. We have seen how social institutions, including the political, which have been intended to serve us as social beings, can be dominated by 'principalities and powers', unleashing various forms of injustice. Drawing on prophetic memory and imagination, and facing the dawn of the kingdom of God, we welcome our liberation, our total salvation. Rebellious powers are unmasked and dethroned, and the clue to our struggle for political justice is given in the cross and resurrection of Jesus Christ. We do not resist evil with evil, but with efficacious love and patient suffering by which we witness to the transfiguration of politics. We have a fore-taste of God's gift of *shalom* and we keep hope alive in the struggle, with the confidence that God will right wrongs in his moment and we shall overcome.

9 Ethics and Salvation*

Duncan B. Forrester

I remember, years ago, some leading members of a congregation with which I was involved were asked to talk at evening services about what Christianity meant to them. One elder spoke about his work for the church. From his late teens he had helped with the Sunday school and had become an NCO in the Boys' Brigade. He had been the youngest elder elected for many years. He had acted as Congregational Treasurer, and had served on countless committees and given a large slice of his life to the service of the church. I do not know what impression he intended to convey, but I suspect he wanted young people to follow in his footsteps so that the congregation he had served so faithfully would flourish in the future. He appeared to be somewhat pleased with himself: a recognised pillar of the community who had devoted himself to service and deserved to be respected and admired. He gave the impression that he had earned the gratitude of the church, and given a good return for what he had received.

The next speaker was of approximately the same age, but his presentation was very different. He gave what was in effect a testimony. He told of how he had as a young man done things of which he was still ashamed, as he drifted around without purpose or direction. And then he had fallen in love – or rather, to his immense surprise, a wonderful girl had fallen in love with him. He could not really understand why, because he did not have much of an opinion of himself. The girl had brought him to church where, once again to his surprise, he found he was accepted

* © Duncan B. Forrester 1994

and quickly felt at home. And then he gradually discovered to his amazement that he knew that he was accepted and loved by God. He did not say anything much about what he was doing, because he did not really think it important, certainly not in the light of the love he had so unexpectedly experienced. He did not give the impression that he thought he had earned anything. Indeed he was constantly surprised by the love and respect with which he was surrounded. But the congregation knew of his quiet, modest work with tough youngsters drifting around the streets. They knew that he would often appear after work, still in his overalls, to redecorate pensioners' tenement rooms. They knew how loved and respected he was within and far outside the congregation for his modesty, his integrity, his openness to people and his joy. As far as he was concerned, his behaviour was not important. It was simply the natural, unself-conscious way for someone who had received so much to behave.

The first speaker suggested that he was saved by his works, his goodness, his ethical behaviour. The second was so surprised and delighted to be loved and accepted that he was quite unself-conscious about the 'good works' that he did. They just flowed from him spontaneously.

Listening to these two men speaking reminded me of Jesus' parable of the Pharisee and the publican – the Pharisee who trusted in his own goodness and accordingly despised those who were less obviously 'good', and the publican, the person of no reputation, who trusted in God and was realistic about his own failures and sin (Luke 18:9–14). The problem with taking the ethical life seriously and struggling to be good is that it so often degenerates into Pharisaism. If we allow ourselves to see our behaviour as something that could earn us our salvation, it in fact leads us away from God. The search for goodness can be a subtle form of sin, making us obsessed with ourselves, punctilious in our behaviour, but not open to God or to our neighbours in gentleness and love.

This is the commonest misunderstanding of the Christian gospel – that it is primarily or centrally about striving to be good. It is often suggested that people go to church as a kind of public demonstration that they are good, that they have arrived, that they have earned peace with God. When this happens the gospel, the good news, has been changed into law, and self-righteousness appears as a parody of true goodness. The change is a perversion which is subtle and often difficult to detect. American 'televangelists', for example, preach a gospel that claims to be evangelical, and verbally it is just that. But the pervasive suggestion that money sent to support 'this Christian ministry' ensures that prayers will be said for the donor and in some strange way money will ensure one's acceptance by God corrodes and disguises the message of grace. Or again, politicians and others are constantly suggesting that the role of the Church is to be a kind of moral policeman, keeping people in line and providing sanctions for traditional morality. In all this kind of thinking the understanding of the gospel is profoundly distorted, making salvation a prize for moral achievement, something that people earn, not something that is freely and graciously given to them. This attitude results in women and men being obsessed with themselves and their own moral achievements or failures.

Augustine and Luther often spoke of sin as the state of being *incurvatus in se*, turned in on oneself, dominated by one's own inner workings, striving always to earn through one's behaviour acceptance by God and by one's fellows. The attention is turned inwards; we take ourselves and our condition with profound seriousness, but we are not really open to God or to our neighbours. Our dealings with others are a way of confirming our self-understanding or our standing. The other is in fact being subtly used for our own purposes. This is a recognised and pervasive problem in the caring professions: the maintenance of the carer's self-image as a warm person who can solve the problems of others is sometimes at the expense of the real needs and interests of those being cared for. The people around a mission station in India once said devastatingly of a senior missionary, 'He does not *really* love us. He only loves us in the Lord'! Similarly, C. S. Lewis recounts in his autobiography, *Surprised by Joy*, how his conversion made him far less engrossed with himself and his own inner workings, and more able to turn outwards to God and people. 'One of the first results of my

143

Theistic conversion,' Lewis wrote, 'was a marked decrease . . . in the fussy attentiveness which I had so long paid to the progress of my own opinions and the states of my own mind . . . To believe and to pray were the beginning of extroversion.'[1] And later in his life his love for Joy Davidman drew him ever more fully out of his shell, as recounted so movingly in Brian Sibley's *Shadowlands*, and now in the fine film of that title.[2]

Salvation is not earned by our goodness. It is not a reward for moral achievement. But it is offered to us out of God's love despite our ethical failures and inadequacies. This is basic to a true understanding of salvation *and* of ethics. The coming of salvation sets us free for truly moral action, it elicits real goodness, love and openness.

Consider, for instance, the story of Zacchaeus, the wealthy, corrupt tax collector. The presence of Jesus in his house, the Jesus who says, 'Today salvation has come to this house', elicits from him a spontaneous and generous response. He gives half of his goods to the poor and restores fourfold everything he had gained by cheating people (Luke 19:1–10). And in the story of the sheep and the goats (Matthew 25:31–46) those who are accepted are the ones who respond lovingly and spontaneously to the needs of their fellows, without thinking of rewards or achievement. They did not know that in doing so they were serving the Lord. They had been set free to serve and love the needy stranger and in so doing they were in fact serving the Lord. Those who are rejected argue that if they had known that the Lord was in the neighbour then they would have helped – precisely because there was something in it for them, they could expect a reward. But they were not in fact taking the needy stranger seriously. They were *incurvati in se*, unable to rise above selfishness to generosity.

But we *are* accepted, we are saved by grace while we are still sinners. And this consciousness sets us free to act well. Faith necessarily 'becomes active in love'. But, as Luther put it, 'we do not become righteous by doing righteous deeds, but having been made righteous we do righteous deeds'.[3] People who know themselves to be saved are able to act in a disinterested way, serving God and neighbour for their own sakes, not to earn anything for themselves. Salvation does not destroy morality; to the contrary, it enables people to be truly moral. To quote Luther again:

> ... when some say that good works are forbidden when we preach faith alone it is as if I said to a sick man: 'If you had health, you would have the use of all your limbs, but without health the works of all your limbs are nothing'; and he wanted to infer that I had forbidden the work of all his limbs; whereas on the contrary I meant that he must first have health which will work all the works of all the members. So faith also must be in all works the master workman or captain, or they are nothing at all.[4]

Another, even more apt, analogy might be the charismatic school teacher whose attitude to her pupils, whom she treats as intelligent, responsible and moral people, elicits from them good behaviour and enthusiastic study. They try to live up to her estimate of them; her care and confidence in them elicits from them far better things than if they were constantly berated for their stupidity and intimidated by the holding before them of impossibly high standards of behaviour and intellectual achievement. Salvation, in other words, elicits and enables ethical activity. It is not a reward for being good.

Salvation is for Christians something that has happened in the past, something that is happening now, and something that will reach its culmination in the future. Achieved historically on the cross, it is being worked out in the present, and is a blessing which will be fully enjoyed at the end of time. The past, the present and the future tenses are used of salvation in the New Testament. Each of these tenses represents an important dimension of the reality of salvation. The verb is usually in the passive mood: we have been saved, we are being saved, and we will be saved. Salvation is not something we do. We cannot save ourselves or others – although remember that the paralytic let down through the roof was healed by the faith of those who bore him there, to Jesus. Salvation is something done for us or to us. Then we may respond, it is true. But salvation is not a command, an imperative, or a call to action so much as a statement in the

145

indicative about something that has happened, is happening and will happen fully in the future. Salvation, for the Christian, is the enabling context within which we act; it is a context which sets us free to respond in love and generosity to our neighbours near and far. The man who replied to the rather impertinent question 'When were you saved?' by saying, 'I was saved two thousand years ago, on the Cross of Calvary', was affirming a fundamental truth about the Christian understanding of salvation. Martin Luther was making a similar point when he cried out at times of turmoil and temptation, *'Baptizatus sum'* – 'I have been baptised'. In his baptism he had died and risen with Christ, he had been incorporated into something that had happened long before, he knew he had been accepted, loved, forgiven. The salvation that has happened in the past is complete, accomplished. We have nothing that we can, or ought to, add to it. The victory has been won and we enjoy its fruits. The battle does not need to be fought again; the result was decisive and permanent.

But that does not mean that we should not respond in joy and thankfulness and celebration to what has been done for us, for God's unbelievable generosity. Those who know that the Son of Man came not to be served but to serve and to give his life as a ransom for many, are called to respond in joyful and thankful service of others (Matthew 20:28; Mark 10:45). The salvation that has been achieved in the past elicits moral behaviour and provides a model of how we should behave. According to John's Gospel, at the meal which prefigured the death that Jesus was to die and expressed its significance, Jesus played the role of the lowest servant, taking a towel and washing his disciples' feet. They protested, of course, but Jesus replied, 'If I then, your Lord and Teacher, have washed your feet, you also ought to wash one another's feet. For I have given you an example, that you also should do as I have done to you.' (John 13:14–15). The true response to knowledge of our salvation is a willingness to pour out our lives in humble, loving service and generosity.

Salvation is also an ongoing reality. We are being saved; we are constantly, as it were, appropriating the fruits of what has been accomplished in the past, inheriting and enjoying the benefits of what has happened. The great hymn in Philippians 2 about Christ's self-emptying and taking the humble form of a servant to die on the cross is sandwiched between two ethical passages, to which it is in fact the key. Before the hymn, believers are urged to be in harmony with one another, to be humble and unselfish, and concerned for the good of others – following the example of Christ. After the hymn this behaviour is understood as 'working out your own salvation with fear and trembling' (v. 12). We cannot view our salvation in a detached or academic way; it calls for a response. It requires to be worked out in practice, and to work its way into the warp and woof of life. And then, as if aware of the danger of thinking that our salvation is something that we *do*, or something that we earn, the writer adds, 'for God is at work in you, both to will and to work for his good pleasure' (v. 13). Salvation shapes our lives and our action, but we do not prove or achieve our salvation by how we behave. Yet the behaviour of Christians should direct attention away from themselves to the Lord and what he has done, it should point towards a salvation that has been achieved and is constantly on offer to all: 'Like a lamp, you must shed light among your fellows, so that, when they see the good you do, they may give praise to your Father in heaven.' (Matthew 5:16). And our Father is the one who forgives and receives us, for those who are saved are still sinners, albeit forgiven sinners, and even the best of their actions only ambiguously reflect the glory of God and God's salvation.

The New Testament also speaks of salvation as a blessing which will be fully enjoyed only at the last, a process which reaches its culmination at the end. It is interesting that all the great images of the fullness of salvation which will be enjoyed at the last are collective, social. Salvation is not an individualistic affair, 'the flight of the alone to the Alone'. It is the conviviality and joy of the kingdom of God, of the city that has foundations, of the new Jerusalem, 'coming down out of Heaven from God, prepared as a bride adorned for her husband' (Revelation 21:2). It is a matter of fellowship, of restored relations, of reconciliation, of people at peace with one another and with God.

Christian ethics is about ways of living in the future today, of living by the standards of the new Jerusalem here and now. That's why it is important that the Beatitudes, which in some ways look so much like a New Testament revision of the Ten Commandments, are not imperatives at all. They are statements about the attitudes which are characteristic of God's kingdom, a picture of what the new Jerusalem is like – a society in which the weak and the poor, the despised and the failures are at the centre of attention. This picture of a new society is, Christians believe, an accurate account of what God has in store for us, the fullness of salvation. And although the kingdom is not fully here as yet, it is possible in action that is loving, just and gentle to anticipate a little of the life of the coming kingdom – a kind of appetiser, and also an earnest (*arrabon*) of the kingdom. The life of the Christian community should be an authentic and winsome – even if partial, fragmentary and preliminary – expression of the life of the kingdom, of the consummation of salvation that is in store for us.

The coming kingdom – and the lives of those who already live the life of that kingdom – is inevitably in tension with the way of the world. And the kingdom is a standing challenge to the inbuilt tendency of all forms of social, political and economic order to claim finality for themselves.

The Christian understanding of salvation therefore nourishes hope, a hope of a better future, a hope of the fullness of fellowship which is promised in the gospel. In the eleventh chapter of Hebrews, at the start of the great rollcall of the heroes of faith who lived by hope, we are told that 'faith gives substance to our hopes'. Faith, in other words, gives shape to hope and sustains hope. This is particularly important in a society which seems to have lost a vivid social hope. When Bishop Lesslie Newbigin returned to Britain after decades as a missionary in India he was asked what was the most dramatic change he noticed in his homeland. 'The disappearance of hope,' he replied. Even in the worst slums of Madras hope that things can be better flourishes; but in Britain, he said, hope has all but vanished. I think Bishop

Newbigin has put his finger on the central problem of our society today. Public, shared hope has withered, and with it the sense of common purpose binding us together has been eroded.

The journalist Jeremy Seabrook, in a remarkable book *What Went Wrong?*, reports on a series of interviews with elderly people who had been active in the Labour movement in the 1930s and 1940s, and, in some cases, back in the 1920s.[5] A common pattern emerges strongly. Year after year it was hope of a more just future that kept these people going, that made hardships, sacrifices and struggle appear worthwhile. Their hope for a better, fairer, more fraternal society was usually shaped and sustained by chapel or kirk, by a faith they embraced, or a faith they fought, believing it had betrayed its deepest insights.

Hope and expectation peaked in the 1940s. Just over fifty years ago the Beveridge Report was published. This became the central pillar of the welfare state and was hailed by the Archbishop of Canterbury as the first attempt to embody the whole spirit of the Christian ethic in an Act of Parliament. What vast hopes were invested in Beveridge's project! When the time came for implementing this shared hope in the late 1940s, a whole generation echoed Wordsworth:

> Bliss was it in that dawn to be alive,
> But to be young was very heaven!

Then, in the late 1970s, when Seabrook spoke to his hopeful ones, now old, he found a pervasive disillusion: the fulfilment, they said, is a parody of what we hoped for, struggled for, planned for; corrosive and pervasive materialism has produced a mockery of all we fought for. Public hope, they believed, had withered and now people, who talk as if happiness can be bought, tell us that this is the best possible life. Rampant individualism has corrupted community.

The chapel and the kirk quietly decline, obscured by the supermarkets which are the shrines of the consumerist society. Consumerism has trivialised and eroded human hope more effectively than materialist philosophy. One of the younger generation, who have deserted the chapels,

149

once seedbeds of hope, told Seabrook, 'I can think of these places only with revulsion. They taught such an austere and unloving view of life. To me, they are symbols of repression, sexual repression and social control. I am pleased to see them in a state of ruin. I exult in it. To me this represents a triumph for humanity.'

A triumph for humanity? Or is it, perhaps, a sign of the collapse of hope – the cutting of the tap-root that down the generations has kept hope alive?

And on the global scene there has been a similar withering of public hope. Think of the vast investment of expectation in the Marxist project, the hope that social justice could be achieved and an earthly paradise established by basic, revolutionary economic change. Alisdair MacIntyre, back in the 1950s, saw Marxism as the repository of hope: Ernst Bloch proclaimed that Marxism was the only heir and modern expression of the biblical tradition of hope.[5] Then came the momentous events of 1989, when the Communist dictatorships collapsed in quick succession from their own internal corruption, leaving behind an abiding suspicion of social hope, of what is sometimes called 'tragic utopianism'. Hopes for the future that have decayed and become diabolic are replaced by a resurgence of old antagonisms and the revival of historic bitterness. It must be hard for a Bosnian Muslim not to despair these days.

From the bosom of the US State Department, the only superpower left, Francis Fukuyama proclaims that history is at an end. There is nothing left to hope for. We have arrived. The absolute moment is here. The triumph of liberal democracy means that there is nothing further to strive for, no possibility of criticising our consumerist society. All that is left is to fine-tune heaven. A faith that gives substance to our hopes is now redundant. A Church that disturbs the present for the sake of a city that is to come is a useless irritant. The hopes of the past have turned sour, bitter and poisonous. We are better off without them. And so a new world order is proclaimed, to freeze and protect the absolute moment, the end of history, at which we have arrived.

The end of history is a comforting notion for the rich and strong. The present ordering of things, they feel, is natural and proper. Now is the moment of truth, when we see that we live in the best of all possible worlds. The only way of helping our fellows, the theorists of this position suggest, is to enrich ourselves. Effortlessly, without any making of sacrifices, the benefits of prosperity will trickle down to the poor. Great wealth alongside grinding poverty is part of the givenness of things. We are reassured, perhaps, when we are told that attempts to help the poor lead remorselessly first to paternalism and then to tyranny – the search for social justice is, it is suggested, 'the road to serfdom'.

So the end of hope is a dungeon for the poor and power-less. The beggars in our streets, the increasing numbers who sleep rough in cardboard cities, the army of the long-term unemployed, the youngsters driven from their homes and now denied benefit all find that they are locked into their predicament by a society that has ceased to hope for sal-vation, for God's future.

I recently took part in a conference on Youth Homeless-ness. We were reminded that in our society a third are pushed to the margins of things and deprived of hope. Two-thirds find hope outdated in the culture of contentment. But in the global scene the proportions are reversed: two-thirds are poor and powerless; one-third are at ease at the end of history. For millions the debt-bondage of Third World countries breeds despair and fatalism.

Still, in a society which has lost its grip on social hope, has ceased to seek a city, the Christian faith stands in all its obvious frailty and weakness as more than an empty husk of spent belief and unfulfilled expectation. It still gives shape to hope and sustains hope even here. The culture of content-ment in a secular society is haunted by the Christian hope.

This is a hope that strengthens and comforts the weak and the poor. Those who have been marginalised and forgot-ten in our society have a special place in the city that is to come, a place of honour where their worth is affirmed. Here there is a home for the homeless, here the isolated and despised find love and acceptance. The weak and powerless take possession of a kingdom which has been prepared for them since the world was made.

This is a hope that disturbs the comfortable. It calls us to

151

account. For nations and individuals will stand before the throne of the Son of Man and answer for how they have treated the hungry, the thirsty, the stranger, the prisoners, the naked – the needy ones with whom the Son of Man chooses to identify himself. The hope is good news to the poor and the rejected and the oppressed, and also to those who respond to them with love and generosity and imagination. Hope is necessary to sustain caring, outreach and the search for justice and community.

This is a hope that rouses the complacent, those who have settled down to enjoy life at the end of history. Abraham, no doubt, was very comfortable in Ur of the Chaldees – prosperous, confident, secure. God called him to journey in hope into the unknown future, seeking a city with firm foundations, whose architect and builder is God.

People who are grasped and captivated by this hope are restless folk, people who ask questions, people on the move, people who serve others, build fellowship, seek justice. They are exiles and strangers on earth, longing for a better country and living the life of that country here and now. 'That is why God is not ashamed to be called their God for he has a city ready for them.' (Hebrews 11:16)

In an age when social hope threatens to disappear because people no longer believe salvation to be necessary, the mighty are left unchallenged and the weak in despair. Only faith in the God and Father of our Lord Jesus Christ can sustain and shape our hope that the salvation definitively manifested in Christ, and constantly invading life, will be finally consummated in the city that has firm foundations, whose architect and builder is God.

10 Salvation and Feminism*

Beverley Clack

Personal reflections

It is very difficult for me to think of a time when Christianity
and feminism (although I would not necessarily have been
aware of that term) have not been part of my experience.
My Christian background has left me with a sense of the
God who is to be found in the creation, the God who has
sanctified and hallowed human flesh through the incarnation. My feminist beliefs find their basis in my childhood
and my feeling that there was no reason why I as a woman
should not have the same opportunities as men have to
decide how to live my life. On several occasions I was upset
to discover that not everyone thought as I did when it
came to these issues of equality! As I grew older I was able
to name my fundamental belief in sexual equality as 'feminist'. But it is fair to say that both my Christian beliefs and my
feminist ideals have developed and grown from childhood
responses to the nature of reality.

It must be said, however, that I have found it easier to
maintain a feminist position than a straightforwardly Christian one. My Christian faith is constantly open to interpretation and often revision. And it is precisely within the area
of soteriology that my Christianity has had to be subjected
to the most rigorous feminist critique: what sense can I, as
a feminist, make of the claim that the man Jesus Christ is
saviour? Whilst some might see feminism as a concern that
is irrelevant or even inappropriate to issues of salvation, I
have come to recognise an intimate and essential connection

between feminist principles and the idea of 'salvation' or, as I would name that fundamental concern with freedom, 'liberation'.

Salvation and women

Many women feel 'saved' by the message of feminism from the drudgery of labour which is 'woman's work', and from false stereotypes of what it means to be a woman. The mass media provides apparently endless advertisements which rest on an idealised form of female beauty. The ideal woman is shown as white, slim, young, wrinkleless and characterless. She is both submissive and alluring. As Naomi Wolf has pointed out, women are sold a myth of feminine beauty which saps both energy and resources. Women worldwide spend more than £12 billion per year on beauty products; a figure which is even more shocking when one realises that women in general are poorer than men.[1] The pursuit of a fantasy of beauty is not, then, a trivial matter. It takes up much time and money. Responding to this situation, feminism reacts against the claims of manufacturers and advertisers that there is one idealised idea of female beauty. The message that feminism proclaims in the face of media stereotyping is controversial: women should be accepted as they are, not forced to conform to any particular stereotype of what it is to be female. Feminism affirms women as individuals; it denies any stereotypical understanding of what it is to be a woman. For many women, myself included, the message of feminism is contained in one word – freedom.

Are feminist understandings of the nature of salvation at odds with Christian claims for salvation through Christ? Feminists like Mary Daly and Daphne Hampson have rejected Christianity because they believe that its message of the 'God-Man' is one which both alienates and oppresses women. To begin with, I shall share some of those ideas, notably the claim that the Christian account of salvation through Christ is dependent upon a negative understanding of humanity and specifically of the nature of woman. However, I believe that Christianity and feminism are not mutually exclusive, and I shall go on to offer some reflections on the Christian message as 'liberation', showing a possible connection between feminist and Christian ways of thinking about freedom.

Salvation and sin

The Christian understanding of salvation can be viewed as offering a bleak account of the world and humanity, for the concept of sin is intimately connected with the hope of salvation. In traditional Christianity there has been a tendency to interpret 'sin' in a narrow, individualistic way. Whilst its broader meaning focuses upon the claim that humanity has 'turned away' from God, there has been a tendency to focus upon sexuality in particular and sensuality in general as the prime source of sin. This has had particularly damaging consequences for women. Within the Christian tradition, women have been equated with sexuality, with the flesh, with the natural created order. As Rosemary Ruether points out, in the Gospel of the Egyptians Jesus declares, 'I have come to destroy the works of the female'[2] – that is, sexual desire and procreation. The 'Fathers' of Orthodoxy, such as Augustine, viewed women with suspicion as sexual beings who were likely to lead good, spiritual men astray:

> What is the difference whether it is in a wife or mother, it is still Eve the temptress that we must beware of in any woman.[3]

Leaving aside such narrow conceptions of the sin that humans need to be saved from, another major strand within the tradition has understood sin as selfishness. This has also proved problematic for women. Care of the self, thought for the self, 'self-centredness', have all been seen as the root of godlessness. Yet for many women the sin has not been selfishness but the lack of any clear self-identity in the first place. The Christian emphasis on selflessness has in many cases exacerbated the problem. The martyr in the home, frustrated, unable to feel anger at her lot, has been perpetuated by a theological approach which views the self with suspicion. In order to understand fully the implications of self-denial, one must first have a sense of one's self. Too often a message which might rightly challenge the self-centredness of men has been misappropriated by women.

A consideration of the Christian account of sin would be incomplete without some reference to the story of Adam and Eve. At the heart of the traditional Christian message of the need for salvation from sin has been the story of the Fall in Genesis 2:4–3:24. This story more than any other has been responsible for some of the most damaging sexual stereotypes of women. According to this story, sin enters into human life when Eve is tempted by Satan in the guise of a serpent, and, in defiance of a divine command, eats from the tree of knowledge of good and evil. This act of disobedience has ramifications for humanity in general (death enters into human experience) and for woman in particular (she is to be subordinate to man).

The main focus of the story, which affects all human beings, concerns death. Death is now part of human experience. It is this linking of death with sin that has had considerable implications for the Christian message. Augustine, writing in the fifth century, understands death as the direct result of sin:

> The first men were so created that if they had not sinned, they would not have experienced any kind of death; but that, having become sinners, they were so punished with death, that whatsoever sprang from their stock should also be punished with the same death.[4]

Accordingly, salvation has been understood primarily as the defeat of death orchestrated by the sacrificial death of Christ. Whilst this message expresses the hope that God and life will overcome wickedness and death, it can be given a more negative rendition. Salvation can – falsely – be understood as referring to an event which takes place *after* death. If salvation is understood as taking place in a world other than this one, it becomes tempting to view this world as unimportant, as something to be used or abused, rather than revered as in some sense holy. As we near the end of the twentieth century, we are faced with a hitherto unprecedented ecological crisis. Christianity cannot shirk its responsibility for perpetuating a mindset that has failed to see the world as the realm of God's activity.

If death is the result of sin for all humanity, woman is

doubly cursed. The sin of Eve is one which must be paid for by all her daughters. Following the Fall, the hierarchy of relationships which is implicit in the creation of Eve from Adam's rib is made explicit. The curse on Eve reads thus:

> To the woman he said, 'I will greatly increase your pangs in childbearing; in pain you shall bring forth children, yet your desire shall be for your husband, and he shall rule over you.' (Genesis 3:16)

Eve's role is specifically linked to her procreative function – an understanding of the nature of woman which has formed the basis for many an argument against women taking active roles outside the home. Her fate is sealed – the man shall rule over her.

It is this part of the story that I wish to focus on, for it is this element in it which has been used to support the claims of patriarchy (literally, 'the rule of the fathers', the form of society which assumes male domination). Male headship is viewed as the only adequate form of leadership. Because of the role she played in the fall of humanity, woman is relegated to a subordinate position. For many feminists, it is the story of the Fall that makes the Christian message impossible to countenance, particularly because the figure of Eve is still used to argue against equality for women. David Pawson's recent book against the leadership of women clearly pointed the finger at Eve:

> Eve, as typical woman, was more liable to be misled and therefore more likely to mislead.[5]

Eve is representative of each woman. Thus it is women, in general, who are to blame for the Fall, and that guilt is to follow women throughout their lives. Moreover, the sin of Eve has been connected with the idea of sexual guilt. The serpent has been understood as the seducer of Eve. Pawson writes that Eve was 'more vulnerable to being seduced in mind'[6] – an interesting use of language! Eve is thus revealed as the archetype for woman as whore. It is in Eve's sexual nature that the source of the Fall is found. Thus sexuality and woman as sexual being are condemned at one and the same time.

157

Despite the negative connotations for women of the way in which sin has been traditionally discussed, I would want to maintain that notions of sin are still important for understanding the human condition. It is at this point that I believe feminist ideas can open up a new and radical understanding of the concept of sin. The tendency to consider sin as an issue relating to individual transgressions in many ways fails to take account of the far-reaching nature of the problem. Sin relates not only to individuals, but to the way in which relationships within society are constructed.

According to feminists, the sin which underpins all others and which is itself established in the Genesis story of the Fall is the sin of patriarchy. By establishing the male domination of human life, hierarchical structures become the defining mark of human society. When Eve is told to submit to Adam, human relationships are defined in terms of unequal power. Domination and hierarchy become factors in human relationships. The patriarchal construction of society legitimates men as the natural rulers over and against women. From this fundamental distinction between men and women develop all other hierarchical understandings of the world: white/black, rich/poor, master/slave. This sin which leads to hierarchical structures is itself universal, distorting all human relationships. Patriarchy perpetuates ways of thinking which divide the world into 'us' and 'them'. It is this divisive approach to human life that is the root sin, and it is this way of structuring society that we need to be saved from.

In exposing the structural sins of patriarchy and hierarchy I believe feminism makes a significant challenge to the central claims of Christianity. If, according to feminists, male domination and the hierarchies which arise from this phenomenon are what we need 'saving' from, can a *male* saviour achieve this?

The role of Christ

Rosemary Ruether in her book *Sexism and God-Talk* first posed the question, 'Can a male saviour save women?'[7] Much of the feminist critique of religion has been concerned with this question. The figure of Christ is particularly problematic for feminists. Not only is Christ proclaimed as 'the New Adam' who restores the form of humanity lost by the sin of Eve, thus linking Christian understandings of salvation with the misogynistic story of the Fall, but Christian doctrine has also proclaimed Christ to be the revelation of God. It has been tempting for theologians to postulate that because this revelation is male then God too must be male. Jakob Sprenger and Henry Kramer in their fifteenth-century handbook for witchfinders, the *Malleus Maleficarum*, explicitly illustrate this way of thinking. In a passage in which they seek to show why more women than men turn to witchcraft – it is because of the insatiable lust of women – they conclude with thanks to (the male) God:

> And blessed by the Highest Who has so far preserved the male sex from so great a crime: for since He was willing to be born and to suffer for us, therefore He has granted to men this privilege.[8]

Comments like these – and this example is unfortunately not an isolated case – pose a very real threat to my faith. If women can be viewed with such contempt within a tradition, it would seem that any self-respecting woman should leave the Church as quickly as possible. While it is possible to condemn comments like those of Sprenger and Kramer out-of-hand, orthodox Christology itself seems to have little to offer women.

Definitions of Christ and his work have focused upon the meaning of the 'God-Man', seeking to establish appropriate language for speaking of Christ as both divine and human. In many ways, it is this kind of language that has proved to be so problematic for feminists. Once a man is identified as God the Son of God the Father, patriarchal structures can be viewed as divinely ordained. The hierarchical nature of patriarchy reflects the will of the patriarchal God. As Mary Daly has noted in words that I continue to find challenging, 'if God is male, then the male is God'.[9]

But is this the only understanding we can have of the Christian gospel? Rather than rely on the theological fulminations of the theologians of the tradition, we would be well-advised to return to the gospels and the kind of Jesus who is portrayed there. When we read the gospels, we are

159

confronted with a Christ who challenges the validity of many social stereotypes, a figure who dines with prostitutes, who enjoys the company of social outcasts, who refuses to be bound by hierarchical notions of who constitutes the powerful in society. The ministry of Christ reflects the rejection of hierarchical notions of power: only God, the source of all life, demands unconditional devotion. The Christ of the scriptures can be viewed as the liberator, the one who shatters stereotypical understandings of the nature of human relations.

So how are we to understand the significance of Christ if we are to take seriously the feminist critique of theological language which affirms the 'God-Man'? This phrase has the potential to alienate some women. However, when I confess Jesus as the Christ, I am not focusing upon his masculinity or 'manhood'. Rather I am affirming the embodiment of a way of living. Christians are called to live in union with the spirit of the Christ revealed in the New Testament. To call Jesus 'Christ' is not just to make a statement about an historical figure; it is also to confess a messianic way of living in harmony with God and others.

I would not want to be understood as rejecting the importance of the embodied Christ. The significance of Christ lies in the way of life he expresses, but this must be placed alongside an acceptance of the incarnation as the affirmation of the embodied nature of humanity. The idea that the body has to be neglected and denied in order to be 'spiritual' is a travesty of the Christian gospel. At the heart of the Christian message lies the belief in God as the one who embraces all being and affirms the natural as good.

The affirmation of Christ as that spirit which leads us to act in a particular way in the world and the idea of the incarnate God are both established by the commitment to action. The significance of Christ as the spirit we share seeks expression in the way we live. The incarnate Christ affirms the realm of our action as good. Thus it seems appropriate to speak of Christ as establishing the model for liberated humanity; a humanity which is not ashamed of the flesh, or shackled by false hierarchical understandings of human relationships, but is able to act in a Christ-like way in the world.

Liberation and feminism

It is at this juncture that I believe a change from the language of salvation to the language of liberation is necessary. It seems to me that the challenge of feminist thinking lies in the way in which it has exposed the negative understandings of the natural world and the place of humanity within it assumed by much of the language of salvation. Moreover, the language of salvation has been dependent upon the Genesis narrative of the Fall, a story which has been used against women who have been categorised by many of the leading theologians of the tradition as 'daughters of Eve', and thus responsible for the perilous state of fallen humanity. The language of liberation has none of these unfortunate connotations. Indeed, the way in which this word 'liberation' has been used in recent theology is suggestive of a new and exciting approach to the Christian message.

Liberation theology attempts to apply the message of Christ as liberator to situations of poverty and oppression in the world. This methodology, highly influential in Latin America, sees theology as a secondary discipline, a way of speaking which comes after one's commitment to liberating the poor and oppressed.[10] At the same time, the social analysis of the liberation theologians is radical in the true sense of the word; in order to understand the root causes of poverty, one must get beyond a superficial analysis of the situation (for example, ideas that the poor are poor because they are lazy) to a deeper analysis of the real sources of such oppression (that is, the inhuman excesses of capitalism and the global economy).

Liberation in this context refers to the desire that all human beings should be free. In this sense, feminist thought is intimately connected with liberation theology. Feminists claim that all human beings – and that includes those who are often the oppressed of the oppressed, women – should have the freedom *to be*. Daly expresses the feminist commitment to liberation as a commitment to 'the emergence of whole human beings'.[11] This, it seems to me, encapsulates the message of Jesus when he said, 'I have come that they might have life, and life more abundantly' (John 10:10). Feminist theology, like liberation theology, demands a radical analysis of the human situation, and particularly the way in which male domination has warped the message of the Christian gospel. A recognition of this guilt is necessary if we are to move to a new and authentic appreciation of the Christian message as the good news of liberation for all.

In contrast to some accounts which appear to view salvation as something that happens outside time and space, independent of the individual, liberation must be understood as an active concept, involving commitment and responsibility. If we experience liberation we are led to desire it for others. Feminists often talk of the need for 'consciousness-raising', the process whereby one makes other women aware of patriarchal oppression and the need to confront it. Likewise, the life of Christ embodies the divine wish for human freedom. When the liberating word of the Spirit is experienced, we are led to desire such freedom for all humanity, and particularly for those who are the victims of the patriarchal system of hierarchy and oppression.

If the language of liberation is adopted, there will be ramifications for Christian theology as a whole. Notably, the Christian understanding of God must come under scrutiny. If the Christian message is concerned with liberation, the way in which we speak of God may need to be modified. Often God is described in terms which suggest that the key attribute of divinity is power. Too often the understanding of divine power offered within the tradition has justified hierarchical and oppressive understandings of human power. God's power has been understood in quantitative terms, as a power 'greater' than that of any human being. God is God precisely because 'he' is 'all-powerful'. Such a definition of God's power reflects patriarchal concerns with power *over* others. God is God as 'he' is more powerful than even the most powerful world leader. Such an understanding of divine power is at odds with the liberating word 'freedom' for it reinforces hierarchical accounts of the relationship between human beings. In order for someone to be powerful, there have to be others who are less powerful or powerless.

It strikes me as bizarre that this understanding of God's power should have taken such a hold on the Church. The power of God has been defined more in terms of the first Christian emperor Constantine than in terms of the 'power' of Christ. Christ himself seems to have been elevated to the central place of the imperial pantheon. Yet consideration of the New Testament accounts of Christ's ministry reveals a picture which is radically opposed to this notion of power over others as the defining mark of the Godhead. Christ's passion and death reveal a 'powerless' God; at least, that is the case if we define power in patriarchal terms. God is revealed as a God who suffers with human beings, rather than as a God who is in control of the universe, sending suffering as a punishment for sin. Instead of defining God's power in hierarchical terms, a qualitative understanding of power is necessary. God is that spiritual dimension which is translated into liberative action. God's power is not power over humanity. Instead, belief in the power of God expresses commitment to the liberation of others. God is the spirit which *empowers* us in this task. Power, then, can be defined in radically non-hierarchical terms. In developing an understanding of the apparently powerless God revealed in the suffering Christ, and the implications that this concept of God has for Christian solidarity with the sufferer, the sin of patriarchy can be broken. In this sense, Christianity and feminism can be viewed as having a common agenda – the destruction of hierarchy and oppression.

At the same time, the language of liberation can have a wider context than its application to human relationships. It can also be linked to the ecological liberation of the planet. Recent feminist writings in this area have been most illuminating. Writers such as Ruether have suggested that theology has an impact on the way in which human beings view and use the world.[12] If God is viewed as all-powerful, radically opposed to the things of this world, then it is not surprising that human beings have felt free to exploit the world's resources with little consideration for how that affects the environment. If, on the other hand, God is understood through the incarnation as in some sense embodied, sharing in the life of the creation, then the world and the natural realm can be considered sacramentally. The world itself reflects the spiritual dimension.

Feminist theologians have sought to reaffirm the dignity and importance of the body. Traditionally, women have been identified with matter, nature and sexuality while men have been identified with mind, reason and spirituality. Whilst feminists have sought to break down the polarisation of these human qualities, it is also important to affirm those elements which have been viewed negatively within the tradition; in other words, those elements which have been equated with woman. In accepting our place in the natural world, in affirming the sexual dimension of humanity, a different approach to human being is offered. Rejecting the polarisation of these attributes establishes a holistic approach to human being. Human beings incorporate both matter and spirit, mind and body, the rational and the emotional, the spiritual and the sexual. And this understanding of humanity should affect our understanding of the world. To be human is to be a part of the natural world. This is not something to be avoided, in the way that some of the Early Church Fathers sought to deny the life of the flesh in order to find the life of the spirit. Rather this acceptance of our place within the world is something to be accepted joyfully. We cannot escape this world, but must learn to live in harmony with the planet.

Conclusion

Feminist writing in the area of religion has provided much stimulating material which often challenges my understanding of what it is to be a Christian and a feminist. Exploring feminist ideas has forced me to revise my understanding of salvation as the central point of the Christian message, leading me to affirm liberation as the good news of Jesus Christ.

The Christian tradition has little to be proud of when it comes to gender issues. The guilt of the tradition in perpetuating stereotypical views of women needs to be faced and new ways of presenting the Christian message need to be offered. Feminists have shown how the language of salvation has been linked to outmoded accounts of the nature of humanity in general and of women in particular. By employing the language of liberation, such negative connotations can be eradicated while holding to the central message of the gospel – 'freedom'. The use of the language of liberation affects not only our understanding of human relationships, but also our understanding of God and ultimately of our place within the world. Employing the principles of feminism in a broader context than just the important but rather marginalised field of gender relations opens up the message of Christianity in a new and exciting way. Reflection on some of the feminist responses to Christianity leads me to affirm what I believe to be the central message of the New Testament – that in Christ human beings are offered the possibility of a new life, a life where all are given the freedom to be.

11 Salvation and Cultural Change*

John W. Drane

'You cannot step twice into the same river, for other waters are continually flowing on.' The words are from Heraclitus, five hundred years before the time of Christ,[1] but they could have been written yesterday. From primeval rain forests to urban slums, today's world is in a state of constant change. In the past cultural change was usually a slow business, as one generation succeeded another and made its own minor adjustments to social habits and ways of thinking. But now change is neither subtle nor gradual: it is traumatic and immediate. The impact of accelerating cultural change is evident wherever we look, and no matter how fast they run, institutional leaders find it impossible to keep up with new directions that seem to be random and unpredictable, and therefore impossible to control or plan for.

'As the rate of change increases, the complexity of the problems that face us also increases. The more complex these problems are, the more time it takes to solve them. The more the rate of change increases, the more the problems that face us change and the shorter is the life of the solutions we find to them. Therefore, by the time we find solutions to many of the problems that face us, usually the most important ones, the problems have so changed that our solutions to them are no longer relevant or effective ... As a result we are falling further and further behind our times.'[2] Moreover, it is not just that things are changing faster than ever before, but the actual nature of change itself seems to have changed. In the words of transpersonal psychologist Marilyn Ferguson, 'We are living in the change

* © John W. Drane 1994

166

of change . . . the entire culture is undergoing trauma and tensions that beg for new order.'[3]

Cultural change

If culture is about the way people live and relate to each other,[4] then Europeans need look no further than their own continent for evidence of massive change and uncertainty. In 1984, who could have imagined that by the early 1990s the map of Europe would be redrawn, that communism would crumble, ancient ethnic animosities would be resurrected, and much of Europe would be living under a dark cloud of savagery and inhumanity that would challenge accepted standards of behaviour and would witness the spectre of neo-Nazi movements again threatening European culture. So far, western Europe has escaped the worst horrors of the social upheaval in the east, but the collapse of the Berlin Wall did not herald the arrival of a capitalist utopia, nor has the European Community emerged as the solution to all Europe's problems. Economic, social, and political co-operation, let alone union, can seem little more than elusive shadows, and the inability of the Community even to form a common foreign policy in relation to the tragic events being played out on its own eastern borders has only served to highlight a major failure of nerve.

In both east and west, Europe has little clear sense of either identity or purpose, and some are now asking bigger and more disturbing questions. What exactly is 'Europe'? In what sense is Europe an identifiable place? Are these countries bound together only by the fact that for centuries they shared a common history? Does the idea of 'Europe' depend more on religion and ideology than on geography and ethnicity? Was 'Europe' a notion that made sense only while the culture of Christendom provided otherwise disparate nations with a common world-view and values? Can a Europe bereft of such an ideological foundation ever hold together, or will it eventually revert to being what it physically is – just an appendage to Asia?

The USA faces similar questions of national and cultural identity. For forty years, American values and national

167

identity were largely shaped by the perceived threat from the old Soviet Union and its allies around the world. Despite all the rhetoric about upholding traditional American values, what Ronald Reagan once dubbed the 'evil empire' was in effect calling many of the shots in US policy, domestic as well as foreign. Now the USA is forced on to the defensive, trying to redefine its role and identity in the new world order, and it faces the same internal ambiguities as Europe. When the 500th anniversary of Columbus' voyages of exploration to the 'new world' occurred in 1992, Americans had no idea how to mark the occasion, let alone celebrate it, because it raised awkward questions about their cultural identity. Who are the real Americans? Certainly not the Caucasian descendants of European explorers and immigrants, though they still hold most of the power. In reality, Americans are an amalgam of many nations, with native Americans, African Americans, Asian Americans, Hispanic Americans, as well as Caucasians – and others – living together in what, in cultural terms, is an uneasy truce that needs little provocation before the cracks begin to show.

There is exactly the same cultural uncertainty in other places where European travellers have settled. Australia has a great burden of corporate guilt hanging over the entire nation, as its immigrant leaders struggle to come to terms with the way their ancestors systematically destroyed the culture of Aboriginal Australians. As recently as the 1960s, state governments were sending raiding parties into aboriginal homelands to kidnap children to be brought up by white city dwellers and integrated into what was supposed to be a more civilised culture. It is still not uncommon to find white residents who think of themselves as Europeans first, Australians second, and Asians not at all. European settlement of New Zealand began more auspiciously with the Treaty of Waitangi (1840) guaranteeing land rights to the original inhabitants, but that was soon discarded by white settlers who now regret it, though they are not consumed with the deep guilt of their Australian counterparts and can at least use their country's original name of Aotearoa. Exactly the same process, with much more suffering along the way, is taking place in South Africa.

While people of European descent look within to patch up their own failing vision, the world centre of gravity is moving elsewhere. The economic power of the west has been declining ever since the Second World War, though the inherited wealth of the previous five hundred years made it possible for westerners still to imagine they were truly in control of things. Today that is no longer the case. The majority of the world's people have always lived in the two-thirds world. Now their influence is growing commensurate with their numbers. The Pacific rim is the world's economic powerhouse, and we can expect other parts of the two-thirds world increasingly to take responsibility for setting the agenda in the next century and beyond.

The influence of the two-thirds world is not just economic, however. It has its own rich cultural heritage which the west is being forced to recognise, not least in relation to religious belief. The rise of so-called Islamic fundamentalism is one of the most obvious expressions of a culture that is different from contemporary western values, though the extent to which this is a 'threat' to the west has been over-rated by the western media, which is generally militantly anti-Muslim.[5] In even more countries, Christianity is a major force. Secular westerners may find it hard to believe, but in world terms Christianity is not declining, but growing very rapidly. As westerners question and reject their traditional faith, the ever-increasing populations of the two-thirds world are embracing Christianity in vast numbers. Some sixty per cent of all the world's Christians now live in the developing world.[6] Even the Christian missionary enterprise is rapidly moving into reverse gear as Christians travel from places like Africa and South America to share their faith in the traditional Christian heartlands of Europe, North America and Australasia.[7] Alongside the shift in the world's economic centre of gravity from the west to the Pacific there is another great shift in the centre of gravity of the Christian faith. For its first thousand years, Christianity was the faith of the Mediterranean lands where it originated. During its second thousand years, it was the faith of people in Europe and the lands to which they emigrated. At the beginning of its third millenium, Christianity is without question the faith of the people of the two-thirds world. That has already led to the emergence of distinctive ways of life, as Christians have been forced to wrestle with the realities of life for those who are poor and marginalised, and have begun to ask what kind of cultural ethos will accurately reflect the message of Christ in such circumstances.[8]

Christians and western culture

If Christianity is growing fast in other parts of the world, why does it apparently have so little to offer the changing culture of the west? The answer to that question is bound up with the Church's role in the development of modern western culture. To understand what Christian salvation might mean in the present context of upheaval and change, we need to review, however briefly, what has been going on in western thinking over the past few centuries.

Before the voyages of people like Columbus, Europeans held a simple world-view that was rooted in the dim mists of ancient history. The earth was a flat disc, and the centre of the universe. Underneath was the world of the dead, up aloft was heaven, and as long as God was in heaven, all was well. Keeping God there was a matter of doing the right things in the right places at the right times, and consequently religion permeated the whole of life. For peasant farmers, sowing seeds and other agricultural operations had religious overtones, and for politicians, national strategies were invariably bound up with religious observance.

The discovery that Europe was less than half the world was a shock to people who had known nothing else, and the success of the explorers provided a major impetus to others who threw themselves with great energy into the search for new light on other hitherto unknown aspects of human existence. When Copernicus (1473–1543) concluded that the universe must be heliocentric, not geocentric, and when the Italian astronomer Galileo (1564–1642) then popularised the idea, they found themselves on a collision course with the establishment. But the new view prevailed, a concept that had been held since the beginning of time was discarded, and there was a paradigm shift of massive dimensions that merely gave permission to others to ask further questions. New discoveries were made at breathtaking speed. Barriers began to fall in every area of human understanding. Great advances in knowledge of the physical universe became everyday occurrences. Following the lead of René Descartes (1596–1650) and Isaac Newton (1642–1727), scientists explored and articulated 'laws of nature' that would give a coherent explanation for things that previously seemed semi-miraculous – and another major paradigm shift in human understanding was under way, this time concerned with the nature of knowledge and what is worth knowing. The age of the rationalist-materialist was about to dawn. In due course there was the development of medical science, along with the Industrial Revolution, the development of technology, and the invention of modern forms of transportation. As 'new worlds' were opened up, the developing self-confidence of the European Enlightenment was spread far beyond its own continent. And so was born that phenomenon we now call 'western culture' or 'modernity': a total world-view and way of life that would ultimately – for good or ill – leave no part of the globe wholly untouched by its influence.

Alongside the scientific and technological achievements, new philosophical and religious concepts played an increasingly significant role. The discoveries that catapulted humanity from the medieval world into the modern age had not been revealed by divine intervention: they emerged over time as human reason was applied to life's ultimate questions, in the search for 'scientific' answers. In that light, it seemed obvious that modern people could live quite happily without the assistance of superstition and mythology (including religion) to explain the meaning of life. In due course, the barriers of the physical world itself were broken, and a man was sent into space. When Yuri Gagarin returned from his historic space flight in 1961 and proudly declared that he had seen no sign of God up there, that seemed to be a fitting epitaph for any kind of religious world-view. Given the time, money and expertise, nothing now seemed impossible. When scientists could give precise answers to

171

every question, who needed God as a means of explaining things?

Looking back, it all seems deceptively simple, if not quaint and idealistic. For even as Yuri Gagarin circled the earth with his confident message of western technology come of age, storm clouds were gathering which in the following thirty years would radically change the contours of much of the western cultural landscape. Today, the heady optimism of the past has been swept away. The old certainties of the Enlightenment are no longer secure, and there is a widespread feeling that science and technology have ultimately failed to deliver the goods. The values of modernity are being questioned at every level, both pragmatic and ideological. No one would wish to turn the clock back, of course, or deny the usefulness of the advances in human knowledge there have been in the last two or three centuries. But more attention is now focusing on the negatives, and the foundational concepts of the whole Enlightenment vision are being subjected to radical questioning. From a scientific angle, the old Newtonian paradigm was challenged by Einstein's theory of relativity as long ago as the 1930s. But its mechanistic model for understanding everything, from people to the cosmos, still continued to dominate long after its theoretical base had been eroded. In conjunction with the thoroughgoing application of a reductionist approach to knowledge, it has created problems and discontinuities in every area of life, from the depersonalisation of modern scientific medicine to the pollution of the environment.

Perhaps more than any other single factor, it is the environmental issue that has led to the questioning and rejection of the old scientific paradigm. People had always assumed that science and technology gave us the power to determine our own destiny. Of course, it was recognised that such power could be used to both good and bad effect. But in the past, it seemed possible to undo or forestall any harm that might occur. In the days of the cold war, we all knew the potential danger of nuclear holocaust, but there was the unspoken assumption that, being people of common sense and rationality, the leaders in both Kremlin and White

House would see the futility of pushing the button and would therefore desist from doing so. We were right: human reason did prevail. But the environmental crisis is not susceptible to that kind of resolution. We have now unleashed forces that no amount of human reason will be able to control. For the first time since the Middle Ages people see their ultimate future destiny lying in the control of unknown, and probably unknowable, natural forces. Human reason enabled us to know how to make holes in the ozone layer, but it cannot tell us how to patch them up again, and as a result we may yet be fried alive in our own lifetime. Whether or not that doomsday scenario comes to pass, there is little we can do about it. The great promise of Enlightenment science was that it would enable us to control our environment, rather than the environment controlling us. Now that possibility looks to be slipping away, it increasingly seems that the rationalist-materialist-reductionist outlook can no longer supply satisfactory answers to today's most urgent question.

So what has gone wrong? Has something important been lost during the past few centuries? There is an insistence in many circles that nothing less than another radical paradigm shift will suffice, this time abandoning the mechanistic models of the past to adopt a more holistic view of things. 'In contrast to the mechanistic Cartesian view of the world, the worldview emerging from modern physics can be characterised by words like organic, holistic and ecological. The universe is no longer seen as a machine made of a multitude of objects, but has to be pictured as one indivisible, dynamic whole whose parts are essentially inter-related and can be understood only as patterns of a cosmic process.'[9] Such talk of inter-connectedness at once raises questions that are of an essentially spiritual or mystical nature. Physicist Fritjof Capra makes the connection quite explicitly, claiming that the new holistic paradigm will be 'similar to the views of mystics of all ages and traditions'.[10] Instead of searching for rational explanations for everything, then, should we not be looking for 'spiritual' solutions to the crisis in our culture? Instead of trusting our logic, would it not be wiser to depend more on our intuition? Questions like that can be uncomfortable for people who have been educated to believe that human reason has the answer to everything and the way to understand things is by taking them to pieces to analyse them. It is precisely as a result of our over-dependence on analytical thinking for so long that western culture now has no idea where to look for spiritual or emotional direction.

The problem is exacerbated by the fact that the traditional western source of spiritual guidance – the Church – is a part of the old cultural establishment that seems to have created our present predicament.[11] It is debatable whether Christian values shaped the Enlightenment, or whether the Church allowed itself to be taken over by essentially secular values, but either way the practical outcome is the same: if Christianity is part of the problem it cannot also be part of the solution. Management professor Russell Ackoff openly states that we will not successfully make the transition from the Machine Age to the Systems Age unless we jettison Christian belief.[12] Consequently, the only place to look for spiritual guidance will be either other cultures and world-views or within ourselves – and both these are playing a significant part in the rising culture.

For some, it leads to the adoption of Asian spirituality, especially Buddhism, or even Islam.[13] For others, it involves rediscovering and accepting native cultures that were displaced by European invasions of the Americas, Australasia or Africa, all of whose people seem to have been able to live at peace with themselves and their environment in a way that we are unable to do. This particular route to a new world-view also has the advantage of facilitating the expiation of some of the west's corporate guilt about its past treatment of these cultures. Yet others find a solution in what is effectively a reversal of history, by jumping backwards over the Christian period into the pagan past of Europe itself, to embrace and affirm the long-lost values and world-views of our own ancestors. Others again seek solace in transpersonal psychology, encouraged by the apparent similarity between its techniques and the experience of mystics through the ages.[14] As a result, a dazzling and bewildering array of different spiritualities compete for attention, each of them claiming to offer something that will help us find our souls again and chart a safe course into the new culture of the future. The goods on offer in this religious market-place range from messages from spirit guides and extra-terrestrials, to neo-paganism, celtic mythology and aborigi-nal spirituality – not to mention renewed interest in astrol-ogy and a vast range of psychological therapies, all holding out the prospect of a renewed, holistic humanity.

Inevitably, the post-modern culture that is now rising in the west is quite different from what preceded it. At one and the same time, it combines an acceptance of many of the fruits of science and technology with a rejection of the world-view that produced them, and what looks like a return to something similar to the ancient spirituality of the pre-critical age. It therefore poses a far-reaching challenge to many accepted cultural norms, not least the notion of objec-tive truth and the role of reason in establishing truth. Bhag-wan Shree Rajneesh summed it up neatly with the claim that 'It is not that the intellect sometimes errs; it is that the intellect is the error'.[15] That is a massive challenge to western life as we have known it. On the one hand, it can manifest itself in the actions of someone like Charles Manson, who could butcher several people and insist that nothing had really happened because on a holistic world-view 'all is one' and so there is no such thing as good or evil.[16] On the other, it might emerge as a revisionist account of Nazi history, in which the holocaust never took place, or, for that matter, in a rewriting of ancient Celtic Christianity to make it more amenable to contemporary New Age spirituality.

The observer who simply wants to know what is going on will not find understanding all this easy, not least because the cultural and intellectual goalposts are being moved all the time. The term New Age 'Movement' is a misnomer, because it makes it sound like the work of a minority pres-sure group. Whatever is happening is certainly much bigger than that and is here to stay. But the term 'movement' does capture the fluid and dynamic feel of things, and explains why some people refuse to take it seriously as a real cultural movement. Ernest Gellner articulates the feelings of many with his wry comment that 'Postmodernism is a contemporary movement. It is strong and fashionable. Over and above this, it is not altogether clear what the devil it is. In fact, clarity is not conspicuous amongst its marked attributes', though he does not miss the key fact that '. . . the notion of objective reality is suspect – all this seems to be part of the atmosphere, or mist, in which postmodernism flourishes, or which postmodernism helps to spread.'[17]

Salvation for the rising culture

What relevance does Christian salvation have for the situation in which we now find ourselves? Put another way, what does the gospel have to say in this context? Asking questions is the easy part. Answering them will be a challenging, even painful, business for the Christian Church. We cannot ignore the repeated claim that the western Christian tradition as we know it is part of the problem and is therefore unlikely to be part of the solution. Some of the negative things being said about Christianity are certainly either untrue or exaggerated. But there is more than just a hint of truth in most of them, and repentance will be a more appropriate response than self-justification, especially in relation to such matters as the pollution of the environment under the influence of the Calvinist work ethic, the exploitation of women, children and native populations around the world, and the perpetuation of unjust and often racist systems of government. Before Christians can channel salvation into the lives of others, they will need to rediscover for themselves the renewing power of God's Spirit: 'the call to conversion should begin with the repentance of those who do the calling'.[18] This applies to evangelisation as well. For here too, the ways in which we now worship and witness seem to be part of the problem, which means that doing more of the same will resolve nothing.[19]

'The medium is the message', and the way Christians have communicated their message has often betrayed the good news they claim to have. There have been dissenting voices in every generation, but from the time of Constantine's conversion onwards the western church has generally allowed itself to be used as a channel for secular culture, rather than critiquing prevailing assumptions by reference to gospel values.[20] When imperialist expansion was high on the western cultural agenda – whether at the time of the Crusades, or the conquest of South America, or the nineteenth-century missionary movement – our forebears needed an imperialistic God and the Church was not slow to supply the need. All too often, 'salvation' was the sharp end of a sword. Even today, when that is no longer literally possible, our evangelistic efforts often have a macho image reminiscent of Hollywood movies at their worst. Arrogance has its own reward, and by being pliable the Church can become enormously rich and influential, as it was during the period of Christendom. The only problem is that the gospel is not about a God who became an all-conquering monarch, but a God who became a child. The first disciples felt uncomfortable about that, and it has caused problems for power-hungry church leaders ever since. The Christian message is not about transcendence and power, but about weakness, vulnerability and powerlessness.

Taking the implications of that seriously will make a significant difference to many aspects of Christian witness in today's world. It relates to the kind of language we use about God, the structures we tolerate in our churches, the way women, men and children of different life experiences find acceptance and affirmation among us, not to mention our styles of worship, the ways we teach and expect people to learn – and even the designs we adopt for church buildings. Being faithful to the gospel vision will also bring us into conflict with certain aspects of post-modern culture, notably its tendency to underplay the reality of evil. For alongside the 'pick-and-mix' approach to spirituality, our culture also has a supermarket mentality about life-styles, in which people choose to be who they are. 'We create the realities we experience ... The universe ultimately gives us what we ask for ... Since we construct our own lives it is false and misleading to blame others for what we are experiencing. ...'[21] That can sound like good news to middle-class western yuppies but it is bad news to the poor and the oppressed, in our own society as well as the rest of the world, and it is completely at odds with the teaching

177

of Jesus, who on encountering those who were sinned-against had compassion on them.

What is the Christian answer? We will certainly need to insist on the objective reality of evil and suffering in the world (no doubt as part of a wider insistence on the existence of objective reality in general). But we should also ask what sin really is. It is easy for Christians who are comfortable to define sin as something that other people do and of which they therefore need to repent. That has often been the starting point for evangelisation.[22] But a message that starts by putting people down will never be good news. Nor is it the message of Jesus, who always lifted up those who were wounded and broken, and whose primary call was to 'Follow me'. It was in the following that disciples discovered the enormity of sin – and their part in it – and realised the need for personal repentance and radical change. In biblical terms, sin is about a breakdown of relationships, not only between people, but between people and the natural environment, as well as people and God.[23] To view sin in exclusively personal terms is theologically shallow and inevitably leads to a deviant view of salvation, with the accompanying conclusion that the gospel is a commodity to be marketed, rather than an all-embracing truth that challenges the whole of life.

There are also important questions relating to the part the Church might play in channelling salvation to our culture. One of the major contemporary trends is the emergence of so-called 'designer life-styles', as people seek identity and satisfaction not from employment but from leisure. There will be fewer and fewer full-time jobs, and whether by necessity or choice people will need to take responsibility for designing their own life-style package. They will increasingly do things because they want to do them, and they believe in them, not because they are expected to do them. Coupled with early retirement and unemployment, that will mean more and more people looking around for causes to which to commit themselves.[24] Many will find themselves attracted to what Christianity seems to be about, but how easy will it be for the Church to accept them? Businesses are already well aware of the need to maximise the support of everyone who relates to their products, including suppliers and consumers as well as their own employees, and have created structures capable of receiving feedback and input from these so-called 'stakeholders'.[25] Churches, however, tend to be closed organisations. Some present so many hurdles to be negotiated before acceptance is achieved that it is a wonder anyone at all ever makes it.

The assumption seems to be that God works only in the Church. But God is at work in the world all the time, and always has been. To believe otherwise is to have a very strange view of God. Theories about salvation only translate into experiences of salvation when Christians recognise what God is doing out there and get alongside God and other people, and in the process 'give an account of the hope that is within them' (1 Peter 3:15). That involves listening to others, as well as speaking with them. It means resisting the temptation to think of ourselves as packagers and marketers of a religious product which people may take if they want (they typically don't). It means taking the incarnation seriously, and ourselves becoming childlike in order to enter the kingdom. It means building bridges towards other people who are not yet believers, facing the challenge of Jesus' question, 'Who are my friends?' (Matthew 12:46–50). It means putting people before programmes. On a personal level (and most threateningly of all, perhaps) it means recognising that we have something to share with other people not because we are different from them, but precisely because we are no different. Their concerns are ours and we stand in solidarity with them because of our humanity. But we see things the way God sees them and that is what makes a difference.[26]

Finally – and perhaps most challenging of all – the Church faces some hard questions about its attitude to the supernatural, the mystical and the numinous. Our evident embarrassment in this area is one of the legacies from the old rationalist-materialist paradigm. But with the rising tide of hands-on spiritual experience in our culture, a non-supernatural notion of salvation is unlikely to serve us well, and if we persist with it we will only succeed in marginalising Christian faith even further. We need to affirm the importance of reason as a God-given faculty, while acknowledging that there is a non-rational dimension to salvation that is not the same as the irrationality for which so many seem to be opting. It will not be easy, if only because we will have to overcome our own inhibitions first.

One of the most encouraging verses in the Bible is Matthew 28:17. Its significance is usually overshadowed by what follows, the 'Great Commission', a passage that over the centuries has had more than its fair share of imperialistic misrepresentation. What precedes it undermines all that, for Matthew records that 'When [the disciples] saw [Jesus] they worshipped him, even though some of them doubted'. Faced with the challenge of taking the gospel to their own culture, the disciples' starting point was their own weakness. They were people with at least as much doubt as faith, who were prepared to take their message on to other people's territory not to conquer it, but with an overwhelming sense of their own inadequacy and vulnerability. No one can read the New Testament and fail to be inspired by their achievement: they were the most successful generation of evangelists there has ever been.

But they knew what we easily forget: that with God, ordinary people can accomplish extraordinary things. The Church is growing in the two-thirds world today largely through the apparently unspectacular witness of ordinary Christians, often children and women. If we could bring ourselves to learn from them, that would be really good news, not only for the Church but also for the wider culture which is desperately searching for new direction and in which we are called to bear witness to our faith.

Conclusion

Donald English

Salvation is clearly not a simple and straightforward matter. But it has certain recognisable elements, and the preceding chapters have hinted at their nature and reality:

There is a God who is willing to save. If the world needs to be saved and is unable to save itself, then God's will and ability to do so are fundamental. For the Christian, God's willingness and capacity to save are spelled out in the life, ministry, dying, rising and ascending of Jesus Christ. That story is told in scripture, formulated in our theology, and reflected and acted upon in the history of the Church. So our earliest chapters dealt with Bible, theology and history.

Yet salvation does not involve simply knowing that there is a God who wishes us to be saved and who is willing to save us. Each of us, and all of us, are invited and required by God's love to take up that gracious provision of salvation, in a setting where other options are attractively present and where the tendency is not to accept God's grace. In that setting God uses the Church as a model of what salvation means, since it is composed of those who recognise their need to be saved and are seeking to live a life in which they have been saved, are being saved, and by God's grace will be saved. So our next chapters were on the sacramental life of the Church, on ways in which it serves the community for Christ's sake, and on its commitment to spread the good news about Jesus in its evangelistic activity.

None of that activity takes place in a vacuum, however. The life of the world neither sits waiting for the Christian witness, nor formulates its ideas on the basis of Christian theology and practice. It seeks an internally meaningful system of its own, based on observation, experience,

181

reflection, and formulation of patterns and principles to regulate and order daily living at individual, corporate and cosmic levels. Any Christian witness has to take account of that reality and address the issues arising there. The section of our book reflecting this reality could have been inordinately long! Instead some chapters point in that direction, in such areas as sociology, ethics and feminism. The examples chosen are meant to be simply examples, with the encouragement to readers to develop reflections in other areas too.

What is clear is that the practice, embodiment and proclamation of salvation through Jesus Christ must occur with a constant awareness of what is happening in the world around us. The final chapter set out some of those realities and hinted at many more. People can only be reached across the middle ground where the scenery, locations and routes are changing all the time.

Christians are called to be disciples of Jesus Christ, whom the writer to the Hebrews described as 'the same yesterday, today and forever'. In a world which is constantly changing, and with increasing speed, this requires great flexibility, holding firmly to the truth once delivered to the saints while discovering its relevance in a world of which the saints never dreamed. My hope is that this book may provide some help in facing that task.

On the wall of a gymnasium in a school at Ibillin, between Haifa and Nazareth, is a frieze depicting scenes from John's Gospel. The frieze looks as though the painter ran out of paint – or time: there are no heads on any of the bodies. I asked Father Elias Chacour, the great disciple of peace in that divided part of the world, through whose energies this school had been built, why this was so. 'The artist deliberately left it like that,' he told me. 'The stories only come to life when the watchers put their own heads on to the bodies.'

We who have written this book invite the readers to carry the story forward.

References

Introduction

1. Paul Kennedy, *Preparing for the Twenty-First Century* (Harper-Collins, 1993).
2. As an introduction to this theme, see Lesslie Newbigin *The Other Side of 1984* (WCC, 1983).

2 Salvation and the New Testament

1. Some commentators would not be so clear about this. There has been a long debate about whether the Greek word used, *katoptrizomenoi*, means 'beholding in a mirror' or 'reflecting in a mirror'. But Paul is summing up a conclusion drawn from a story about Moses in Exodus 34, where 'the skin of his face shone because he had been talking with the Lord'. Because the people were afraid of the 'glory' on his face he put on a veil, which he removed each time 'he went in before the Lord to speak with him'. Paul refers to this in the words, 'when one turns to the Lord, the veil is removed' (2 Corinthians 3:16). So Moses becomes the 'type' or 'pattern' of Christian believing, as is observed by Richard B. Hays in Chapter 4 of his book *Echoes of Scripture in the Letters of Paul* (New Haven, Connecticut: Yale University Press, 1989). Clearly Moses' face reflected the glory of the Lord which he beheld. So the word must capture both ideas.
2. Early Jewish mystical traditions throw light on what Paul means. Such texts speculate about the human form that appears on God's throne in certain key biblical passages like Ezekiel 1. They accept that 'no-one can see God and live' (Exodus 33:18–23), yet 'the appearance of the likeness of the Glory of the Lord' is manifested in this human form. Alan F. Segal, in *Paul the Convert: The Apostolate and Apostasy of Saul the Pharisee* (Yale University Press, 1990), suggests that Paul is our best

evidence that such mystical traditions already existed in the first century. Paul identified the risen Christ with the 'man' seated on God's throne, the glorious image of God. Associated with such visions – and Segal argues that Paul actually had such experiences (see, for example, 2 Corinthians 12:1–9; 1 Corinthians 15:8; Galatians 1:15; together with the Acts accounts of the conversion) – was the idea of transformation. This would explain the importance of being 'glorified' or 'transformed from glory to glory' in both Romans 8:30 and 2 Corinthians 3:18. See also the previous note: Moses reflected the 'glory' he had seen.

3. See further my book *The Theology of the Pastoral Epistles* (Cambridge University Press, 1994).

4. Telling my own story in *Face to Face* (2nd edition, T. & T. Clark, 1990) was an object lesson in the integral and inseparable association of fact and interpretation, especially where one has come to understand one's story in terms of biblical paradigms of vocation.

5. For further information, see my books *The Making of the Creeds* (SCM, 1991) and *The Art of Performance* (Darton, Longman & Todd, 1990).

6. Would that the translation 'have dominion over' (Genesis 1:26 and 28) had never erroneously encouraged exploitation and the neglect of ecological responsibility!

7. I often wish that the nineteenth century had not overlooked Ecclesiastes 3:19–21.

8. Romans 8:22; see Chapter 3 of my book *Can these dry bones live?* (SCM, 1982, 1992).

9. Hans Frei, in *The Eclipse of Biblical Narrative: A Study in Eighteenth and Nineteenth Century Hermeneutics* (New Haven, Connecticut: Yale University Press, 1974), began the movement towards 'narrative theology' and the retrieval of 'story' from the demands of criticism. Northrop Frye, in *The Great Code: The Bible and Literature* (New York and London: Harcourt Brace Jovanovich, 1982), initiated discussion of the literary character of the Bible and its story, so long obscured by historical criticism.

10. The interesting suggestion of E. P. Sanders (in, for example, *Paul and Palestinian Judaism*, SCM, 1977) that Paul did not move from 'plight' to 'solution' but from the 'solution', namely Christ, to recognition of the desperate state humankind was in, is particularly illuminating. It is the sequence of the argument in Romans which obscures this, he suggested, and it

should not be taken as the sequence in which Paul came to his views.

11. *Murder in the Cathedral* (Faber & Faber, 1935; 1982 reprint), p. 19 *et al.*

3 Salvation and Theology

1. See Paul V. Mankowski, SJ, 'Academic Religion', in *First Things* (May 1992), pp. 31–7; quote at p. 34.
2. T. E. Yates, 'Anglicans and Mission', in S. Sykes and J. Booty (eds), *The Study of Anglicanism* (SPCK, 1988), pp. 429–41; quote at p. 441.
3. Adrian Hastings, *A History of English Christianity 1920–1985* (Collins, 1986), pp. 662–3.
4. Basil Mitchell, *How to Play Theological Ping-Pong* (Hodder & Stoughton, 1990), p. 34.
5. I argue the case for giving increased emphasis to church-based theologians in my *The Renewal of Anglicanism* (SPCK, 1993).
6. A rare exception is found in Colin E. Gunton and Daniel W. Hardy, *On Being the Church: Essays on the Christian Community* (T. & T. Clark, 1989).
7. *The Truth Shall Make You Free: The Lambeth Conference 1988* (Anglican Consultative Council, 1988), Resolution 44, p. 231.
8. Ibid., p. 32.
9. Peter L. Berger, *A Far Glory: The Quest for Faith in an Age of Credulity* (New York: Free Press, 1992), pp. 10–11.
10. Ibid., p. 12 (emphasis in original).
11. For what follows, see the analysis in Alister McGrath, *Bridge-Building: Effective Christian Apologetics* (Inter-Varsity Press, 1992).
12. See Ernest Becker, *The Denial of Death* (New York: Free Press, 1973).
13. For the best discussion of this idea currently available, see Harvey M. Conn, *Eternal Word and Changing Worlds* (Grand Rapids: Zondervan, 1984).
14. This tension is superbly explored by Lucien Goldmann, *Le dieu caché: étude sur la vision tragique dans les Pensées de Pascal et dans le théâtre de Racine* (Paris: Gallimard, 1976).
15. For a study, see Alister E. McGrath, *Luther's Theology of the Cross: Martin Luther's Theological Breakthrough* (Blackwell, 1985).
16. For a detailed exploration of this important issue, see Joanna McGrath and Alister McGrath, *The Dilemma of Self-Esteem: The Cross and Christian Confidence* (Wheaton, Illinois, USA and Cambridge, UK: Crossway Publications, 1992).

17. See John Macquarrie, *An Existentialist Theology: A Comparison of Heidegger and Bultmann* (Collins, 1973). For some qualifications of this analysis, see the careful analysis provided recently by Gareth Jones, 'Phenomenology and Theology: A Note on Bultmann and Heidegger' in *Modern Theology* 5 (1989), pp. 161–80.
18. See Alister E. McGrath, '*Theologiae Proprium Subiectum*: Theology as the Critic and Servant of the Church', in W. P. Stephens (ed.), *Festschrift for James Atkinson* (Sheffield Academic Press, forthcoming).

4 Salvation and Church History

1. ARCIC II, *Salvation and the Church* (Anglican Consultative Council, 1987), p. 9.
2. J. Kent, *The Unacceptable Face* (SCM, 1987), p. 44.
3. H. A. Oberman, *Luther – Between God and Devil* (Fontana, 1993), p. 123.
4. For recent introductions see: E. Cameron, *The European Reformation* (Oxford University Press, 1991); S. Ozment, *Protestants, the Birth of a Reformation* (Fontana, 1993); A. E. McGrath, *Reformation Thought – An Introduction* (Blackwell 1988); J. Bossy, *Christianity in the West. 1400–1700* (Oxford University Press, 1985); E. Duffy, *The Stripping of the Altars* (New Haven, Connecticut: Yale University Press, 1993).
    Older studies of Luther are still valuable, e.g. P. S. Watson, *Let God be God* (Epworth, 1947); E. G. Rupp, *The Righteousness of God* (Hodder, 1953); B. Drewery in H. Cunliffe-Jones (ed.), *A History of Christian Doctrine* (1978), pp. 311ff.
5. NB. McGrath, op. cit., pp. 87–119. Cf. H. A. Oberman, *Masters of the Reformation* (Cambridge University Press, 1981); A. E. McGrath, *Luther's Theology of the Cross* (Blackwell, 1985) and *Iustitia Dei. A History of the Christian Doctrine of Justification*, 2 vols (Cambridge University Press, 1989–93).
6. Cf. McGrath, *Theology of the Cross*, pp. 95–8; E. G. Rupp and B. Drewery, *Martin Luther (Documents)* (Arnold, 1970), pp. 5ff.; M. A. Noll, *Confessions and Catechisms of the Reformation* (Apollos, 1991), p. 94; W. J. Cargill Thompson, *Studies in the Reformation* (London, 1980), pp. 60ff.
7. H. Chadwick, *Augustine* (Oxford University Press, 1986), pp. 107ff.; H. A. Oberman, *The Harvest of Medieval Theology* (Cambridge, Massachusetts, 1963), *Forerunners of the Reformation*

(London, 1967), *Masters of the Reformation* (op. cit.), *The Dawn of the Reformation* (T. & T. Clark, 1986).

8. For a modern classic see R. Niebuhr, *The Nature and Destiny of Man*, 2 vols (Nisbet, 1943).

9. Oberman, *Luther*, op. cit., pp. 155ff.

10. A classic account is A. Nygren, *Agape and Eros*, 3 vols (English translation, SPCK, 1939); cf. R. M. Brown, *The Spirit of Protestantism* (Oxford University Press, 1965), p. 55.

11. Preface to the *Letter to the Romans*. This passage was probably read at the meeting in Aldersgate Street on 24th May 1738. I have tried to remove the exclusive language! Cf. P. S. Watson, *The Message of the Wesleys* (Epworth, 1964), p. 8; H. Bett, *The Spirit of Methodism* (Epworth, 1937), pp. 27ff.

12. Oberman, *Luther*, op. cit., p. 80, p. 206.

13. K. Stendahl, *Paul Among Jews and Gentiles* (SCM, 1976); E. P. Sanders, *Paul and Palestinian Judaism* (SCM, 1977) and *Paul* (Oxford University Press, 1991), pp. 33–76; J. A. Ziesler, *Pauline Christianity* (Oxford University Press, 1983), *The Meaning of Righteousness in Paul* (Cambridge University Press, 1972); Commentaries on *Galatians* (Epworth) and *Romans* (SCM).

14. Ziesler, *Pauline Christianity*, op.cit., pp. 84–7.

15. Sanders, *Paul*, op. cit., p. 49.

16. Ziesler, *Righteousness*, op. cit., p. 163, p. 212. Cf. V. Taylor *Forgiveness and Reconciliation* (Macmillan, 1941); B. Drewery in Cunliffe-Jones, op. cit., p. 324.

17. Cf. R. N. Flew, *The Forgiveness of Sins* (Epworth, undated), p. 23.

18. F. Greeves, *Theology and the Cure of Souls* (Epworth, 1960), p. 69.

19. John Betjeman, *Collected Poems* (Murray, 1979), p. 105.

20. D. Davie (ed.) *The New Oxford Book of Christian Verse* (Oxford University Press, 1981), p. 81.

21. Rowan Williams, *The Wound of Knowledge* (Darton, Longman & Todd, 1979), p. 158.

22. P. Tillich, *The Shaking of the Foundations* (Penguin, 1962); R. Garaudy, *From Anathema to Dialogue* (Collins, 1966), p. 36; cf. R. Bultmann, *Kerygma and Myth* (Collins, 1953), Vol. 1, p. 32.

23. Gonville ffrench-Beytagh, *Encountering Darkness* (London, 1973), p. 254.

24. J. M. Turner, 'John Wesley – Theologian for the People' in *URC Historical Journal* (May 1986); A. D. Lindsay, *The Two Moralities. Our Duty to God and Society* (Eyre & Spottiswoode, 1940); L. Newbigin, *International Review of Missions* (July 1979), pp. 301–312; W. D. J. Cargill Thompson, *The Political Thought of Martin Luther* (Harvester Press, 1984); Colin Morris, *Address*

to the Methodist Conference 1976; D. Davie (ed.), op. cit., p. 250.

25. For the Counter Reformation: A. G. Dickens, *The Counter Reformation* (Thames & Hudson, 1968); H. O. Evenett, *The Spirit of the Counter Reformation* (Cambridge University Press, 1968); J. Hurstfield (ed.), *The Reformation Crisis* (Arnold, 1965), Ch. V 'The Counter Reformation' by H. O. Evenett; Noll, *Confessions*, op. cit., pp. 165ff. (includes the 33 canons on Justification).

26. Cited in N. Sykes, *The Crisis of the Reformation* (Bles, 1938), pp. 162–3.

27. G. C. Cell, *The Rediscovery of John Wesley* (USA: Henry Holt, 1935), p. 361; G. Wainwright, *On Wesley and Calvin* (Melbourne: Uniting Church Press, 1987).

28. Cf. A. M. Allchin, *The Kingdom of Love and Knowledge* (Darton, Longman & Todd, 1979), Ch. 3 'Symeon the New Theologian', and *Participation in God* (Darton, Longman & Todd, 1988). Another Anglican who seems unconsciously 'Wesleyan' is Richard Holloway: cf. *Beyond Belief* (Mowbray, 1981), Ch. 9; *Signs of Glory* (Darton, Longman & Todd, 1982), Ch.5; *Anger, Sex, Doubt and Death* (SPCK, 1992), ch. on 'Anger'.

29. H. Butterfield, *Origins of Modern Science 1300–1800* (Bell, 1949); P. Hazard, *The European Mind 1680–1715* (English translation, Penguin, 1964) and *European Thought in the Eighteenth Century* (English translation, Penguin, 1965); P. Gay, *The Enlightenment*, 2 vols (Weidenfeld & Nicholson, 1970); E. G. Rupp, *Worldmanship and Churchmanship* (Epworth, 1938), pp. 14ff., 'Protestantism and Catholicism after 400 years' in D. Pailin (ed.), *Seventy Five Years of Theology in Manchester* (Manchester University Press, 1980), pp. 102ff. and *Religion in England 1688–1791* (Oxford University Press), pp. 217ff.

30. O. Chadwick, *The Popes and European Revolution* (Oxford University Press, pp. 159ff.; W. R. Ward, *The Protestant Evangelical Awakening* (Cambridge University Press, 1992) and *Faith and Faction* (Epworth, 1993).

31. A. G. Dickens, *Martin Luther and the Reformation* (Edinburgh University Press, 1967), p. 173.

32. D. W. Bebbington, *Evangelicalism in Modern Britain* (Unwin, Hyman, 1989), p. 3.

33. R. Anstey, *The Atlantic Slave Trade and British Abolition, 1760–1810* (Macmillan, 1975); G. F. Nuttall, *The Puritan Tradition* (Epworth, 1967), Ch.8 'The Influence of Arminianism in England'.

34. J. M. Turner, *Conflict and Reconciliation* (Epworth, 1985), Ch. 8 'Methodism and the Oxford Movement'.

35. E. Sullivan, *Things Old and New* (St Paul's, 1993), especially pp. 154ff.; J. H. Newman, *Lectures on the Doctrine of Justification* (Rivingtons, 3rd edition, 1874), pp. 303, 320, 365; W. B. Pope, *Compendium of Christian Theology* (London, 1880), Vol. 3, pp. 27–100.

36. H. Küng, *Justification. The Doctrine of Karl Barth and a Catholic Reflection* (Burns, Oates, 1981); K. J. Kuschel and H. Häring (eds), *Hans Küng – New Horizons in Faith and Thought* (SCM, 1993), pp. 138ff.

37. M. E. Brinkman, 'Justification' in N. Lossky *et al.*, *Dictionary of the Ecumenical Movement* (Geneva: WCC, 1991), pp. 560ff.; ARCIC II, op. cit.

38. A. D. Nock, *Conversion* (Oxford University Press, 1931), p. 211.

39. J. H. Plumb, *England in the Eighteenth Century* (Penguin, 1950), p. 94.

40. Turner, op. cit., pp. 82–8; R. Colls, *The Pitmen of the Northern Coalfield. Work, Culture and Protest 1790–1850* (Manchester University Press, 1987).

41. Holloway, *Beyond Belief*, op. cit., p. 163.

Since I wrote this, J. D. G. Dunn and A. M. Suggate, *The Justice of God. A Fresh Look at the Old Doctrine of Justification by Faith* (Paternoster, 1993) has appeared. Dunn gives a brilliant summary of the biblical view of God's grace freely given, the Covenant relationship and Paul's conversion to the view that Gentiles can fully share it. He sees Luther as the 'discoverer' of justification, which ignores late medieval debate. Suggate shows rightly the relationship (as did Luther!) between justification and justice, and ends with a knock-about anti-Thatcherite polemic which seems simplistic.

Quotations from hymns are taken from *Hymns and Psalms* (Methodist Publishing House, 1983).

5 Salvation and Word and Sacrament

1. Quoted in William A. Graham, *Beyond the Written Word* (Cambridge University Press, 1987) p. 141.

2. Cf. Vatican II, *Dei Verbum*, on Divine Revelation, n.10. See also *The Apostolic Tradition*, Report of the Joint Commission between

the Roman Catholic Church and the World Methodist Council (Methodist Publishing House, 1991), nn.9–21.

3. See M. Richards, 'Servants of the Word, Shepherds of the People', in *The Church 2001* (1982), pp. 186–202, and G. Martelet, *Deux Mille Ans d'Eglise en Question* (3 vols, 1984–90), III, pp. 327–9.

6 Salvation and Evangelism

1. T. B. Kilpatrick in *The Encyclopaedia of Religion and Ethics* (1920), s.v. 'Salvation'.
2. Michael Green, *The Meaning of Salvation* (Hodder & Stoughton, 1965); C. Ryder Smith, *The Bible Doctrine of Salvation* (Epworth, 1941).
3. Ryder Smith, op.cit., p. 74.
4. Alan Richardson, article 'Salvation,' in the *Interpreter's Bible Dictionary.*

8 Salvation and Political Justice

1. John Macquarrie, *Three Issues in Ethics* (SCM, 1970), p. 62. See also his *In Search of Humanity* (SCM, 1982), p. 94, and Frances Young, *Sacrifice and the Death of Christ* (SPCK, 1975), p. 97.
2. John W. de Gruchy, *The Church Struggle in South Africa* (Collins, 1979), p. 218.
3. Sehon S. Goodridge, *The Church Amidst Politics and Revolution* (Bridgetown, Barbados: Caribbean Conference of Churches; Cedar Press, 1977), p. 1.
4. Gustavo Gutiérrez, *A Theology of Liberation* (SCM, 1974), pp. 21–42.
5. Pierre Bigo, SJ, *The Church and Third World Revolution* (Maryknoll, New York: Orbis, 1977), p. 139.
6. Paul Avis, 'The Atonement', in *Keeping The Faith – Essays to Mark the Centenary of 'Lux Mundi'*, Geoffrey Wainwright (ed.) (SPCK, 1989), p. 146.
7. Harvey Cox, *God's Revolution and Man's Responsibility* (SCM, 1969), p. 46.
8. José Miranda, *Being and the Messiah* (Maryknoll, New York: Orbis, 1977), pp. 34–5.
9. See J. de Broucher, *Dom Helder Camara: the Violence of a Peacemaker* (Maryknoll, New York: Orbis, 1970).
10. José Miranda, *Marx and the Bible* (Maryknoll, New York: Orbis, 1974), pp. 162–3.
11. Ibid., pp. 189–92.

190

12. Sehon Goodridge, *Politics and the Caribbean Church* (Bridgetown, Barbados: Cadec, Caribbean Conference of Churches, 1971), p. 9.
13. *Kairos Document, Challenge to the Church: A Theological Comment on the Political Crisis in South Africa* (Geneva: WCC, 1985), p. 13.
14. Ibid., p. 19.
15. Gayraud Wilmore, *Black Religion and Black Radicalism: An Interpretation of the Religious History of Afro-American People* (Maryknoll, New York: Orbis, 1983), p. 227.
16. From Martin Luther King Jr's immortal 'dream speech' at a march on Washington in 1963.
17. Jürgen Moltmann, 'The Cross and Civil Religion' in *Religion and Political Society* (1974), p. 35; cited in de Gruchy, op. cit., p. 222.
18. André Dumas, *Political Theology and the Life of the Church* (SCM, 1978), p. 106.
19. For a good discussion see John H. Yoder, *Politics of Jesus* (Grand Rapids: Eerdmans, 1978), pp. 92–128, 147–61, 248–50.

9 Ethics and Salvation

1. C. S. Lewis, *Surprised by Joy* (Fontana, 1959), p. 186.
2. Brian Sibley, *Shadowlands* (Hodder & Stoughton, 1985).
3. Martin Luther, *Disputation against Scholastic Theology*, Clause 40. *American Edition of Martin Luther's Works*, Ed. J. Pelikan and H. T. Lehman, St. Louis, Concordia and Philadelphia, Muhlenburg Press, Vol. XXXI, 1957 p. 12.
4. Martin Luther, *A Treatise of Good Works*. in *Philadelphia Edition of the Works of Martin Luther*, Philadelphia, A. J. Holman, 1915–32, vol. 1, p. 199.
5. Jeremy Seabrook, *What Went Wrong? Working People and the Ideals of the Labour Movement*. London, Gollanz, 1978.
6. Alasdair MacIntyre, *After Virtue: A Study in Moral Theory*. London, Duckworth, 1981 and *Whose Justice? Which Rationality?* London, Duckworth, 1988; Ernst Bloch, *Atheism in Christianity*, New York, 1972 and *The Principle of Hope*. 3 vols. Oxford, Blackwell, 1986.

10 Salvation and Feminism

1. See Naomi Wolf, *The Beauty Myth* (Vintage, 1990), p. 113.
2. Rosemary Radford Ruether, *Sexism and God-Talk* (SCM, 1983), p. 128.

3. Letter 243:10, quoted in Karen Armstrong, *The Gospel According to Woman* (Pan, 1986), p. 61.
4. From *The City of God*, Book 13, Chapter 3, quoted in R. S. Anderson, *Theology, Death and Dying* (Blackwell, 1986), p. 52.
5. J. D. Pawson, *Leadership Is Male* (Highland, 1988), p. 23.
6. Ibid., p. 23.
7. See Ruether, op. cit., Chapter 5.
8. J. Sprenger and H. Kramer *Malleus Maleficarum* (1486), edited and translated by Montague Sommers (New York: Benjamin Blom, 1970), pp. 44–6.
9. Mary Daly, *Beyond God the Father* (The Women's Press, 1986), p. 19.
10. See C. Boff and L. Boff, *Introducing Liberation Theology* (Burns & Oates, 1987).
11. Daly, op. cit., p. 14.
12. See Rosemary Radford Ruether, *Gaia and God* (SCM 1992).

11 Salvation and Cultural Change

1. Plato, *Cratylus*, 402a.
2. R. Ackoff, *Creating the Corporate Future* (New York: John Wiley, 1981), pp. 4–5.
3. M. Ferguson, *The Aquarian Conspiracy* (Paladin, 1982), pp. 30, 77.
4. On the nature of culture, see Bernard Waites *et al.*, *Popular Culture: Past and Present* (Croom Helm, 1982); Rosamund Billington *et al.*, *Culture and Society* (Macmillan, 1991). And on cultural change, Ivan Brady and Barry Isaac, *A Reader in Cultural Change* (New York: John Wiley & Sons, 1975); Jeffrey C. Alexander and Steven Seidman, *Culture and Society: Contemporary Debates* (Cambridge University Press, 1990).
5. On the western press and Islam, see N. Daniel, *Islam and the West: the making of an image* (Edinburgh University Press, 1960); E. W. Said, *Covering Islam: how the media and the experts determine how we see the rest of the world* (Routledge & Kegan Paul, 1985).
6. For statistics on this, see David B. Barrett (ed.), *World Christian Encyclopedia* (New York: Oxford University Press, 1982), and regular updates published by him in a variety of journals.
7. Current trends indicate that by the year 2000, 55% of all Protestant missionaries will be non-western. Cf. J. H. Kraakevik and D. Welliver, *Partners in the Gospel* (Wheaton: Billy Graham Center, 1992), pp. 161–75.
8. Most notably in the rise of Liberation Theology, though by no

means limited to that. Cf. T. Witvliet, *A Place in the Sun* (Maryknoll, New York: Orbis, 1985); P. Berryman, *Liberation Theology* (London, Tauris, 1987); Robert McAfee Brown, *Liberation Theology: an Introductory Guide* (Louisville: Westminster/ John Knox, 1993).

9. Paul Davies, *Society and the Rising Culture* (Flamingo, 1989), p. 66.

10. F. Capra, *The Turning Point* (Flamingo, 1983), p.xvii.

11. On this, see Capra, op. cit., especially pp. 21–2 where he lists the characteristics of the 'old age' in terms that are too close for comfort to traditional Christian attitudes: 'masculine, demanding, aggressive, competitive, rational, analytic . . .' For a remarkably similar analysis (though from a Christian perspective, and therefore reaching different conclusions), see Lesslie Newbigin, *Foolishness to the Greeks* (Geneva: WCC, 1986); *The Gospel in a Pluralist Society* (SPCK, 1989).

12. Ackoff, op. cit., pp. 19–20.

13. Increasing numbers of western people are converting to Islam, mostly as western women marry into Muslim families, but also significant numbers of Afro-Caribbeans who find themselves alienated by western cultural values, and others who are attracted by the moral demands Islam places on believers.

14. On transpersonal psychology and the emerging spirituality, see R. S. Valle, 'The Emergence of Transpersonal Psychology', in R. S. Valle and S. Halling (eds), *Existential-Phenomenological Perspectives in Psychology* (New York: Plenum Press, 1989), pp. 257–68.

15. Bhagwan Shree Rajneesh, *I am the Gate* (New York: Harper & Row, 1977), p. 18.

16. Cf. R. C. Zaehner, *Our Savage God: the perverse use of eastern thought* (New York: Sheed & Ward, 1974).

17. Ernest Gellner, *Postmodernism, Reason and Religion* (Routledge, 1992), pp. 22, 23. On the New Age more generally, see my *What is the New Age saying to the Church?* (HarperCollins, 1991).

18. *Mission and Evangelism. An Ecumenical Affirmation* (Geneva: WCC, 1982), section 13.

19. On this, and much of what follows, see my *Evangelism for a New Age: creating churches for the next century* (HarperCollins, 1994).

20. The various possible models for the interaction of Christian faith and culture have been well explored in such classic works as H. Richard Niebuhr, *Christ and Culture* (New York: Harper & Row, 1951) or Charles H. Kraft, *Christianity in Culture* (Maryknoll, New York: Orbis, 1979), and in more pragmatic

terms in works such as Bruce J. Nicholls, *Contextualization: A Theology of Gospel and Culture* (Paternoster Press, 1979) and J. R. W. Stott and R. Coote, *Down to Earth. Studies in Christianity & Culture* (Hodder & Stoughton, 1981). But overall it is still much easier to find examples of Christianity allowing itself to be taken over by the prevailing culture, than challenging and questioning it.

21. J. L. Simmons, *The Emerging New Age* (Santa Fe: Bear & Co, 1990), p. 83.

22. It was also the theological foundation on which Thatcherism was built in the 1980s: cf. M. Novak, *The Spirit of Democratic Capitalism* (New York: Simon & Schuster, 1982); D. Anderson (ed.), *The Kindness that Kills* (London, SPCK, 1984); J. Davies (ed.), *God and the Marketplace* (London, Institute of Economic Affairs, Health & Welfare Unit, 1993).

23. For a provocative study of the whole question of sin, see Matthew Fox, *Original Blessing* (Santa Fe: Bear & Co, 1983). Fox raises many questions, and should not be read uncritically, but we will need to grapple with the issues to which he draws attention. For more on Fox, cf. Andrew Deeter Dreitcer, 'A New Creation', in *The Way* 29/1 (1989), pp. 4–12; Ted Peters, *The Cosmic Self* (San Francisco: Harper, 1991), pp. 120–31; Jane E. Strohl, 'The Matthew Fox Phenomenon', in *Word & World* 8 (Winter 1988), pp. 42–7; M. Brearley, 'Matthew Fox: Creation Spirituality for the Aquarian Age', in *Christian Jewish Relations* 22/2 (1989), pp. 37–49; C Noble, 'Matthew Fox's Cosmic Christ – a critical response', in *Crux* XXVII (1991), pp. 21–9; John Drane, 'Defining a Biblical Theology of Creation', in *Transformation* 10/2 (1993), pp. 7–11.

24. Cf. Charles Handy, *The Age of Unreason* (London, Business Books, 1989), pp. 137–402.

25. Cf. Ackoff, op. cit., pp. 25–49; Charles Handy, *Understanding Organizations* (London, Penguin, 4th edition, 1993), *passim.*

26. For more on this, cf. Raymond Fung, 'Mission in Christ's Way', in *International Review of Mission* LXXIX (1990), pp. 4–29; *The Isaiah Vision* (Geneva: WCC, 1992).